P9-EDL-069

WHAT PRINCIPALS NEED TO KNOW ABOUT

Teaching and Learning Reading

SECOND EDITION

A Joint Publication

PATRICIA M. CUNNINGHAM

JAMES W. CUNNINGHAM

Copyright © 2013 by Solution Tree Press

Materials appearing here are copyrighted. With one exception, all rights are reserved. Readers may reproduce only those pages marked "Reproducible." Otherwise, no part of this book may be reproduced or transmitted in any form or by any means (electronic, photocopying, recording, or otherwise) without prior written permission of the publisher.

Visit **go.solution-tree.com/leadership** to download the reproducibles related to this book.

555 North Morton Street

Bloomington, IN 47404

800.733.6786 (toll free) / 812.336.7700

FAX: 812.336.7790

email: info@solution-tree.com

solution-tree.com

Printed in the United States of America

16   15   14   13   12   1   2   3   4   5

Library of Congress Cataloging-in-Publication Data

Cunningham, Patricia Marr.
  What principals need to know about teaching and learning reading / Patricia M. Cunningham, James W. Cunningham. -- 2nd ed.
      p. cm.
  Includes bibliographical references and index.
  ISBN 978-1-936765-53-9 (perfect bound) 1. Reading (Elementary)--United States. 2. Reading (Middle school)--United States. 3. Language arts (Elementary)--United States. 4. Language arts (Middle School)--United States. 5. Elementary school principals--United States--Handbooks. 6. Middle school principals--United States--Handbooks, manuals. I. Cunningham, James W. II. Title.
  LB1573.C795 2013
  372.4--dc23
                                              2012027029

___

Solution Tree
Jeffrey C. Jones, CEO
Edmund M. Ackerman, President

Solution Tree Press
President: Douglas M. Rife
Publisher: Robert D. Clouse
Editorial Director: Lesley Bolton
Managing Production Editor: Caroline Wise
Senior Production Editor: Suzanne Kraszewski
Proofreader: Elisabeth Abrams
Text Designer: Jenn Taylor
Cover Designer: Amy Shock

ACKNOWLEDGMENTS

Solution Tree Press would like to thank the following reviewers:

Nick Ahearn
Principal
Clifford Marshall Elementary School
Quincy, Massachusetts

Sherryl Ahern
Coordinator, Early Childhood and
    Elementary Language Arts
Baltimore County Public Schools
Towson, Maryland

Ronald Collins
Principal
Carpenter Elementary School
Ann Arbor, Michigan

Elie Gaines
Principal
Black Mountain Elementary School
Cave Creek, Arizona

Ann Giddings
Literacy Consultant
Hattie B. Stokes School
Lebanon, Indiana

Adrienne Gideon
Principal
Rosedale Elementary School
Rosedale, Indiana

Michelle Lenarz
President, Ohio Council of the
    International Reading Association
Associate Professor, Department of
    Literacy and Middle Childhood
    Education
Walsh University
North Canton, Ohio

Sharon Mason
Principal
Deep Creek Elementary School
Baltimore, Maryland

Nancy Moga
Principal
Callaghan Elementary School
Covington, Virginia

Keith Polette
Professor, Department of English
    Education
University of Texas at El Paso
El Paso, Texas

Randi Saulter
Education Consultant
Columbus, Ohio

Elizabeth Sturtevant
Professor, Division of Elementary,
   Literacy, Multicultural, and Secondary
   Education
George Mason University
Fairfax, Virginia

Kenneth Weiss
Professor, Department of Reading and
   Language Arts
Central Connecticut State University
New Britain, Connecticut

TABLE OF CONTENTS

Visit **go.solution-tree.com/leadership** to download the reproducibles related to this book.

Reproducible pages are in italics.

FOUR

FIVE

SIX

SEVEN

ABOUT THE AUTHORS

Patricia M. Cunningham, PhD, is a professor of education at Wake Forest University in Winston-Salem, North Carolina. After graduating from the University of Rhode Island, she taught first and fourth grades and remedial reading in elementary grades in Florida and Indiana. After teaching at Ohio University and serving as director of reading for Alamance County Schools (North Carolina), she went to Wake Forest University to direct the Elementary Education program. Pat is the author of *Phonics They Use: Words for Reading and Writing,* currently in its sixth edition. Along with Richard Allington, she published *Classrooms That Work: They Can All Read and Write* and *Schools That Work: Where All Children Read and Write.*

James W. Cunningham, PhD, is emeritus professor of literacy studies at the University of North Carolina at Chapel Hill. Jim has over 100 publications, including books, book chapters, research articles, professional articles, and scholarly reviews. He has spoken at many national and international conferences. He has taught at the elementary and secondary levels and served as a consultant with schools, districts, and other education agencies in twenty-five states. In 2010, Jim was selected as a member of the Text Complexity Committee for the Common Core State Standards in English Language Arts. He is a member of the Reading Hall of Fame.

Pat and Jim met in graduate school at the University of Georgia. In 1977, along with Sharon Arthur Moore, they published their first book: *Classroom Reading Instruction, K–5: Alternative Approaches.* Both Pat and Jim have always been passionate about teaching all children to read and finding alternative ways to teach children for whom learning to read is difficult.

To book Pat or Jim for professional development, contact pd@solution-tree.com.

INTRODUCTION

Long ago, before we knew each other, we both experienced firsthand how important a good principal can be to a school's instructional program. In our fourth (Pat) and first (Jim) year of teaching, we found ourselves in fortunate circumstances: working under the guiding and supportive hand of a leader who saw both teachers and students as people and learners. Jessie Moon of W. T. Moore Elementary School in Tallahassee, Florida, and Paul Braden of South Pittsburg Elementary School in South Pittsburg, Tennessee, were instrumental in helping us become better teachers, in part, because of the vision they shared with us of what a good school looks and feels like.

Many years have passed since then, but we have continued to benefit from time spent in schools with effective principals. As university professors who have had our students intern regularly in classrooms, and as consultants who have worked with hundreds of schools to help them improve their literacy instruction, we have been privileged to watch many principals lead their schools to significantly improve the teaching of reading.

We have written this book for principals who desire to provide the leadership for their school's reading program or are already doing so. The approach we have taken stands on two feet—one set on a large body of research and professional experience in reading; the other set on what we have learned from helping teachers and schools improve their reading programs. We hope you will find this book to be a tool that helps you elevate the teaching of reading in your school, not just a book *about* reading.

In every school, there are individual teachers who provide excellent literacy instruction to all their students. To have effective reading instruction in every classroom, however, requires a schoolwide emphasis on literacy and someone to lead that effort. If you are a principal, assistant principal, curriculum coordinator, reading specialist, or literacy coach, and it is your job to ensure that your school provides effective reading instruction, we wrote this book for you. In the remaining chapters of the book, you will discover what research, experience, and common sense tell us about effective reading instruction and how it translates to best practice.

Chapter 1 focuses on the big picture and what is known about the current state of reading instruction. We explain why reading is considered one of the most complex acts people engage in and how we believe failing to acknowledge this complexity was one reason for the failure of Reading First. Chapter 1 also provides a brief overview of the research on what constitutes effective reading instruction and why this instruction must be carried out in the context of a nurturing, supportive classroom environment. How assessment can hinder or promote good instruction and how the school schedule affects literacy instruction are two other big ideas in chapter 1 that relate to all aspects of effective reading programs.

Chapter 2 is on comprehension because comprehending what you read is what reading is all about. The chapter begins by describing three roadblocks that commonly get in the way of good comprehension instruction. Then it gives you some specific indicators of good comprehension instruction to look for as you look at instruction, lesson plans, and schedules. Finally, it contains the most important information in this book—a list of resources you can use to help your school improve its comprehension instruction.

When we were first asked to write this book, we were reluctant to take it on because we knew there would not be enough space to provide the level of detailed information schools need to carry out state-of-the-art instruction in all the components of reading. (We also knew that even if we had enough page space, few administrators who are responsible for the total curriculum as well as everything else that comprises a school would have time to read a 500-page book!) What good would it do to write a book that helped leaders identify problems and then not provide enough detail so these problems could be addressed? Fortunately, we hit on the idea of including in each chapter a list of books and articles with detailed descriptions and lesson templates that matched the effective instruction we had suggested and that enabled teachers to overcome the roadblocks. This idea came to us just before we left for the International Reading Association national convention in Orlando. At that meeting, we both spent hours in the exhibits looking for resources. Only when we had enough practical resources to provide the rich detail to allow teachers to implement the kind of instruction we advocated did we agree to write this book. If you decide that improving comprehension instruction is a priority in your school, form study groups and use these resources to plan for and implement more effective comprehension instruction.

Because meaning vocabulary knowledge is highly associated with comprehension, it is the focus of chapter 3. In fact, if we know how many of the key words in a text a reader has appropriate meanings for, we can make a good prediction of how well that reader will comprehend that text. We describe roadblocks to and indicators of effective vocabulary instruction. If you decide that improving meaning vocabulary instruction is a priority in your school, you will find the practical, targeted resources for vocabulary study groups very useful.

Chapter 4 focuses on strategies for helping students become better readers of the informational texts they encounter in science and social studies. Most of the reading your students will do in high school and college will consist of informational texts; children who have experienced a steady diet of stories only are often unprepared for the reading demands of academic subjects. The Common Core State Standards acknowledge the importance of informational text by including separate standards for informational text as well as separate standards for reading in academic subject areas.

Phonics is the focus of chapter 5. Phonics instruction is critical for success in reading; however, in the early grades, you have to make sure that phonics is part of a comprehensive reading program that also includes vocabulary and comprehension. You also have to ensure that phonics instruction continues through the upper grades when students need to be taught how to use morphology—roots, suffixes, and prefixes—to decode, spell, and build meaning for the multisyllabic words that make up the bulk of new words students encounter from third grade on.

Many people consider fluency to be the bridge between decoding and comprehension. Fluent reading is reading with appropriate phrasing and expression. In chapter 6, you will find the most blatant example of how assessment can hinder good instruction. In many schools, fluency is measured only by speed, the number of words a student can read correctly in one minute. In this chapter, we describe ways to adapt fluency assessments so that they actually measure fluency as well as strategies for building fluency, and we provide resources for fluency study groups.

The biggest determinant of how well your students read is how much they read. Simply stated, the more you read, the better you read. Children who like to read read more than children who only read when required to. The two activities that have been shown to build intrinsic motivation for reading—teacher read-aloud and independent reading in materials of your own choosing—are the subject of chapter 7.

One striking feature of the most effective teachers is that their classrooms have unusu-ally high levels of engagement and motivation. The three major roadblocks to motivation and engagement, ways to overcome these roadblocks, and study group resources to help teachers increase motivation and engagement in their classrooms are the topics of chapter 8.

Chapters 2 through 8 are focused on how to provide comprehensive, multifaceted literacy instruction in all classrooms. All children benefit from a strong classroom program, but it is particularly important for struggling readers and English learners. In chapter 9 you will find effective ways to provide extra beyond-the-regular-program support to your struggling readers and English learners.

Each chapter from 2 through 9 begins by discussing the roadblocks schools may face in that part of the reading program. Next, the chapter details what you should look for to assess how effectively your school is providing instruction in that area. The final section lists resources we have carefully chosen to help your teachers work together to increase the quality of their instruction in that area if you determine that is a priority in your school.

Finally, we would like to suggest how you might read this book. Begin with the assumption that, in reading instruction as in everything else, no school is perfect! As you read the chap-ters and carry out your observational research, consider how well your school's instruction matches the best practices described in each chapter. Look at your school's comprehension and vocabulary instruction during the reading instructional time as well as in the curriculum areas of science and social studies. Look at how phonics and fluency instruction are included as parts of a comprehensive program and at how fluency is being assessed. Determine the state of teacher read-aloud and independent reading and consider how motivated and engaged your students are in all aspects of reading. Look at the "extra" instruction your struggling readers receive and determine if it is targeted to their needs and truly extra—in *addition to* rather than *instead of.* When you feel you have the big picture of the state of reading instruction in your school, set priorities. What components does your school most need to work on? Which components, while not perfect, are good enough for now?

You will read in the first chapter that the most effective schools and teachers "do it all." But they almost certainly didn't achieve that pinnacle overnight. Work with your teachers to set priorities. Use the resources we suggest to get your study groups thinking and planning. Observe the changes teachers make to the areas you prioritized, and when you are satisfied that the instruction in the component you targeted is moving in the right direction, work on your next priority. You can do it all—and your teachers can do it all—but not this week or this month, and probably not this year!

ONE

BUILDING AN EFFECTIVE READING PROGRAM

Strike up a conversation with anyone about reading, and that person will have an opinion about how we should teach it:

> "Turn off the TV and get rid of the video games."

> "Parents need to read to their children and talk to them."

> "Schools need to cut the frills and stick to the basics."

> "Just teach them good old-fashioned phonics, and they will learn."

Everyone has an opinion and often a simple answer to the challenging issue of teaching reading. As an administrator whose job it is to provide leadership to your school's reading program, you must wade through the opinions (which often include simplistic solutions) to discover, explain, and support a sound reading program in your school.

Most of this book is devoted to describing the roadblocks to good reading instruction, the indicators of effective instruction, and practical solutions to implement in areas in which you determine your school has specific needs. This chapter sets the stage for these specifics by focusing on the big picture and what we know about the current state of reading instruction.

Reading Is Complex

Reading is a complex subject—both to learn and to teach. Adults—who have been reading for so long—often do not realize the many complicated actions that happen in the brain as we read. At the most basic level, our eyes have to focus on the print. We must recognize that the spaces separate words. We have to begin on the left and move across to the right. These eye movements must be learned, and if we were learning to read in another language, such as Chinese, our eyes would move in very different ways.

As we read, we quickly recognize almost every word, pronouncing it aloud or in our minds if we are reading silently. Occasionally, we encounter an unfamiliar word such as *pluvial* and use our phonics knowledge to decode it. Often the unfamiliar word is one we haven't heard before. If *pluvial* is not a word you have a meaning for, you won't know the difference between a pluvial lake and other kinds of lakes unless the text goes on to clarify the meaning of *pluvial*. If you cannot associate meaning for several of the key vocabulary words in a passage, your comprehension will be impaired because associating meanings with words is critical for comprehension. As you are reading, you must also read fairly quickly and give the words the kind of phrasing and expression you would give them if you were speaking the words. This fluent reading allows you to get meaning from phrases of words and promotes comprehension.

Indeed, reading is multidimensional—it requires the brain to perform many functions simultaneously. No matter what kind of text you are reading, print processing, automatic word identification, decoding, fluency, and meaning vocabulary are essential to comprehension. In addition, different kinds of texts require different strategies. Most children read stories better than they read informational texts. Because so much of their reading has been stories, they have learned what is important to pay attention to. Stories have characters and settings and problems to be solved or goals to be reached. Texts that compare and contrast the kind of animal and plant life found in deserts and in rain forests have none of these story features. Nor do texts that explain how the water cycle works or why climate change is an issue we should all be concerned about.

Reading may even be the most complex subject we teach because comprehension is what matters, and comprehension depends on all these parts working smoothly together. The need to learn how to read many different kinds of texts in different subjects adds another dimension of complexity. There can be no simple solution for helping all our students become proficient at the complex task of reading.

Reading First Didn't Work

When No Child Left Behind (NCLB) was passed in 2002, it promised that by 2014, all children would read at grade level. Although NCLB did not require the implementation of specific commercial reading programs, the Reading First component of the legislation did require that reading curricula must be based on "scientific" research. This requirement led almost all schools that received federal funds to adopt one of a few available commercial reading programs. These programs focused almost exclusively on phonics instruction in the early grades; what students read consisted of highly decodable texts with words chosen based on which phonics principles had been taught so far. The programs were also scripted, specifying in the teacher's guide exactly what the teacher should say and how much time should be spent on each part of the lesson. Many school systems, fearful that teachers would deviate from the script, hired monitoring services to ensure fidelity of implementation.

Studies have demonstrated that Reading First was not effective in raising reading achievement scores and that many children were left behind. In the federal government's final report on the impact of Reading First, the evaluators (Gamse, Jacob, Horst, Boulay, & Unlu, 2008) conclude:

> There was no consistent pattern of effects over time in the impact estimates for reading instruction in grade one or in reading comprehension in any grade. There appeared to be a systematic decline in reading instruction impacts in grade two over time. (p. xvi)

The government's official evaluation of Early Reading First (the part of Reading First that applied to preschools) also identified a lack of effectiveness in crucial areas of reading development (Jackson et al., 2007):

> Overall, we find that [Early Reading First] had a statistically significant positive effect on children's print and letter knowledge but no statistically discernible impact on phonological awareness or oral language. (p. xxiii)

In addition, results from the National Assessment of Educational Progress in Reading (NAEP Reading) demonstrate the lack of effectiveness of Reading First. Seven years into the implementation of Reading First and more than halfway to 2014, 33 percent of America's fourth graders scored below the basic level and 67 percent scored below the proficient level. Only 8 percent performed at the advanced level (National Center for Education Statistics, 2010).

Reading First also failed to reduce achievement gaps in reading. The gap between Hispanic and white fourth and eighth graders on the NAEP Reading assessment remained the same in 2009 as it was in 1992 (Hemphill & Vanneman, 2010). Reardon (2011) summarized data that show the achievement gap between children from high- and low-income families was 30 to 40 percent larger among children born in 2001 than among those born twenty-five years earlier.

The failure of Reading First can probably be attributed to two factors: the narrow scope of the instruction and the scripted nature of that instruction. The first main idea of this chapter explains that reading is complex and multidimensional. Consequently, children need instruction in all the components. Instruction in the core programs adopted by Reading First schools was focused almost exclusively on phonics and fluency. Vocabulary and comprehension instruction were largely left until the later elementary years when students supposedly should have already mastered phonics and achieved fluency.

Lesaux and Kieffer (2010) gave a standardized reading comprehension test to 581 urban sixth graders, including both language minority and native English speakers, and found that 45 percent of students scored at or below the 35th percentile. The 262 struggling readers were then tested to determine their relative strengths and weaknesses on the major components of reading. Decoding was above average for 78.6 percent of the struggling readers and a relative strength for the majority of the rest. Fluency was at least average or a relative strength for the majority of struggling readers. What the struggling readers had most in common was low meaning vocabulary knowledge. A study that followed 200 low-income children from preschool to first grade reached similar conclusions (Juel, Biancarosa, Coker, & Deffes, 2003). When the 200 children were evaluated on their decoding and meaning vocabulary skills as they entered preschool, most showed deficits in both areas. The children improved in their decoding skills each year. By the middle of first grade, their average decoding scores were slightly above national norms. In their vocabulary development, however, these low-income children were as far behind (nearly one standard deviation) in first grade as they had been in preschool.

Juel and her associates then looked at their classroom observations and coded all the instruction they observed. The only category of activities that had a positive effect on meaning vocabulary was "anchored word instruction" in which the teachers introduced words focusing specifically on their meanings. First graders who experienced more anchored word instruction had higher vocabulary scores. Conversely, the vocabulary scores of children in classrooms that spent the largest amount of time in letter-sound instruction actually decreased.

This study and others show that the near exclusive focus on phonics and fluency under Reading First was inadequate to prevent readers from struggling or to teach them what they would need to know to be able to comprehend satisfactorily when they reached the upper elementary grades and middle school. Juel concluded her research with one of the best arguments for the need for comprehensive reading instruction right from the beginning:

> Ultimately, effective early reading instruction must help students learn to identify words and know their meanings. With so much research emphasizing the importance of early development in both word reading and language skills, we must consider how to provide instruction that fosters students' vocabulary development without losing the promising results of effective instruction in decoding. It does little good, after all, to be able to sound out the words *pond, mill* and *haystack* if you have no idea what they mean. (Juel et al., 2003, p. 18)

One of the most basic principles of effective instruction is that teachers must tailor their instruction to the needs of their students. In a scripted program, you can't do that, and if you do deviate from the script and one of the watchers happens to be sitting at the back of your classroom, you will be "called down" for your lack of fidelity. Teachers we have worked with have cited many instances of this kind of monitoring. The one that is most egregious and hard to believe unless you heard it firsthand was from a first-year teacher who told us of being marked down on the evaluation for not following the script. Following the script from the manual, he introduced the word *Caribbean* before students read.

A student raised his hand and asked, "Where is the Caribbean?"

This fledgling teacher pulled down the map, located the Caribbean, and then continued the lesson as scripted. He received an unsatisfactory evaluation. Locating the Caribbean on the map was not in the script!

In hindsight, we should not be surprised by the failure of Reading First. In fact, if focusing instruction primarily on only two of the components of reading and doing that instruction in a scripted way had worked, it would have contradicted much that decades of research, experience, and common sense have taught us.

All Schools Can Increase Reading Achievement

Research shows that Reading First did not work, but it also informs us about what does work. Researchers in three studies identified unusually effective teachers and observed them to determine what factors accounted for their effectiveness.

One observational study included thirty exemplary first-grade teachers in five states (Pressley, Allington, Wharton-McDonald, Block, & Morrow, 2001). At the end of the year, each teacher identified six students—two low-achieving, two middle-achieving, and two high-achieving students—and these children were administered a standardized reading test. Based on the results of this test, a most effective and a least effective teacher were identified for each of the five locations. Comparing observations in the classrooms of the most and least effective teachers revealed the following characteristics of the most effective classrooms:

- Teachers explicitly taught decoding skills and related them to reading and writing.

- Books were everywhere and used in a variety of ways—read aloud by the teacher and read and listened to on tape by students.

- Children did a lot of reading and writing throughout the day and for homework.

- Teachers had high but realistic expectations of children and monitored their progress regularly.

- Teachers modeled and expected self-regulation. Students were taught to check and reflect on their work and to make wise choices.

- Teachers made cross-curricular connections. For example, children read and wrote while studying science and social studies themes.

- Classrooms were caring, positive, cooperative environments in which discipline issues were handled quickly and quietly.

- Classroom management was excellent, and teachers used a variety of grouping structures, including whole class, one-to-one teaching, and small groups.

- Classrooms showed high student engagement: 90 percent of the students were engaged in their reading and writing work 90 percent of the time.

The researchers followed up their first-grade study by looking at exemplary teachers in fourth grade (Allington & Johnston, 2002). After observing thirty fourth-grade teachers from five states and examining samples of work and data and interviewing teachers and students, researchers concluded that the following variables distinguished the most effective from the less effective classrooms:

- All kinds of real conversations took place regularly in the most effective classrooms. Children had conversations with the teacher and with each other.

- Teachers constantly modeled thinking strategies. More emphasis was placed on how to find out than on right and wrong answers.

- All kinds of materials were used for reading and writing. Teachers "dipped" into reading, science, and social studies textbooks. Students read historical novels, biographies, and informational books. Magazines and the Internet were used to gather information.

- Word study focused on building interest in words and on looking for patterns in words.

- Learner interest and engagement were important variables in the teachers' planning. Teachers taught the standard curriculum but tailored it to their students' interests, needs, strengths, and weaknesses.

- Managed choice was a common feature in these classrooms. Students were often presented with a topic or problem and allowed to choose which part of it they would pursue and what resources they would use.

- Instruction took place in a variety of formats: whole class, various types of small groups, and side-by-side teaching.

- Students were expected to work collaboratively and take responsibility for their learning.

- Reading and writing were integrated with other subjects. Many of the books students read during reading time were tied to science and social studies topics.

The Center for the Improvement of Early Reading Achievement (CIERA) investigated school and classroom practices in schools with unexpectedly high achievement and compared them to what was happening in similar schools in which students were not "beating the odds" (Taylor, Pearson, Clark, & Walpole, 2000). When comparing the classroom practices in the two kinds of schools, the researchers concluded that the teachers in the schools that were beating the odds:

- Had higher pupil engagement

- Provided more small-group instruction

- Provided more coaching to help children improve in word recognition

- Asked more higher-level comprehension questions

- Communicated more with parents

- Had children engage in more independent reading

In these observational studies of highly effective classrooms, reading instruction was comprehensive and multifaceted and recognized that reading is a complex act. In addition, teachers made instructional decisions and chose materials based on their observations of students' strengths, weaknesses, and interests. They used commercial materials, but none of them based their instruction exclusively on a single core program, and none of them used a scripted program provided by a company that had never met or worked with their students.

These three studies highlight classroom practices that can increase reading achievement, even for struggling students. The next question—and the central question of this book—is how do you as a school leader work to increase the prevalence of such practices during reading instruction throughout your school? As you will see in the remaining chapters, school change in reading requires a clear understanding of the current state of reading instruction in your school and reliance on enhanced teacher expertise as the means to improve. One longitudinal study illustrates how these two factors can be major parts of the solution for a school's less-than-satisfactory reading scores.

Fisher, Frey, and Nelson (2012) recount how Chula Vista, a Southern California K–6 school district with a large percentage of minority learners, significantly increased reading achievement once the small improvement from implementing Reading First plateaued. Before the implementation of Reading First, only two of the forty-four schools in the district met state reading targets. After the core program required by Reading First that included 120 hours of state-approved professional development had been in place for two years, twelve of the forty-four schools were achieving adequate growth, but thirty-two still were not. Dissatisfaction with these results led district leaders to work with consultants to create a more effective program. Even though the proportion of minority students in the schools increased over the time, the initiative they put in place resulted in forty-one of the forty-four schools meeting growth targets in reading!

The program and its implementation had two aspects that mirror the approach we take in this book. First, the specific actions the consultants and school leaders (principals and peer coaches) took to improve schools were based on repeated "schoolwide walk-throughs," "visiting every classroom at a given school," and "looking for patterns across classrooms" (Fisher et al., 2012, p. 552). In each of the subsequent chapters in this book, you will find a discussion of what to look for as you walk through the classrooms of your school, supported by a reproducible checklist to guide your observations of that chapter's component of reading instruction. The purpose of this discussion and checklist is to help you determine how prevalent quality instruction in that area of reading is in your school. Like the schools in Chula Vista, your actions to improve reading achievement are more likely to work if you base them on what is actually happening (and not happening) in your classrooms.

The second aspect of Chula Vista's successful school change effort we want to emphasize was their reliance on teacher expertise rather than instructional materials as the chief means to raise reading achievement. In each of the remaining chapters, you will find a list of carefully selected resources for possible use by your teachers in study groups to increase their expertise in providing instruction responsive to student needs in that chapter's component of reading instruction.

Effective Literacy Instruction Requires a Supportive, Nurturing Classroom Environment

It can be argued that some of the characteristics of effective reading instruction listed in the previous section have more to do with classroom culture than with reading. In the first-grade study (Pressley et al., 2001), the researchers observed that the classrooms were caring, positive, cooperative environments; that classroom management was excellent; and that there were high levels of student engagement. In the fourth-grade classrooms (Allington & Johnston, 2002), students were expected to take responsibility for their own learning, managed choice was a common feature, and teachers considered learner interest and engagement when planning lessons. The researchers at CIERA also noted higher levels of pupil engagement in the most effective classrooms (Taylor et al., 2000).

Researchers at the University of Virginia have conducted a series of studies that demonstrate the importance of an emotionally supportive classroom, especially for children who show early signs of being at risk for failure. One study looked at 910 kindergarteners who had behavioral, attention, academic, and social problems in kindergarten (Hamre & Pianta, 2005). Some of these kindergarteners were placed in first-grade classrooms that offered strong emotional and instructional support. At the end of first grade, these students were achieving at the same level as their low-risk peers. Students who were at risk and placed in less-supportive classrooms had lower achievement and more conflict with teachers. The researchers concluded that:

> Among children at high functional risk (those who displayed some combination of early behavioral, attentional, social, and/or academic problems) academic achievement in the first grade was highest for those in classrooms offering high emotional support. In these classrooms, teachers were aware of and responsive to individual students' needs, offered effective and proactive behavior management, and created a positive classroom climate in which teachers and students enjoyed each other and their time in the classroom. (p. 962)

Like all instruction, reading instruction operates within the culture and climate of the classroom. Educators have long intuited that happy, well-managed classrooms are good for children. We now have data demonstrating that good instruction is not enough for children at risk—being in supportive, positive classroom environments is also required for higher reading achievement.

Assessment Can Promote or Hinder Good Instruction

With the NCLB mandate that reading achievement be measured and scores reported for all subgroups of students, assessment now plays a significant role in reading programs. Assessments help ensure that all students receive instruction and none are neglected; however, they also take up time that teachers would otherwise use for instruction. Assessment promotes good instruction when schools assess with validity the things that really need to be assessed and then make instructional decisions based on those assessments. Assessment hinders good instruction when schools assess merely what is quick and easy to assess. Many of the assessments that consume so much of our instructional time are not leading to better instruction for our students.

For example, in many primary classrooms, students are regularly given a test that purports to measure fluency, such as the DIBELS (Dynamic Indicators of Basic Early Literacy Skills; Good & Kaminski, 2002). Students are provided with a grade-level passage to read and then given a score based on the number of words read correctly in one minute. Based on that score, some students are designated as at risk for reading failure. Jay Samuels (2007), a recognized expert on automaticity and fluency in reading, states the problem with this assessment:

> Despite their labels, [the DIBELS tests] are not valid tests of the construct of fluency as it is widely understood and defined. They only assess accuracy and speed. By attaching the term fluency to their tests, they create the false assumption that that is what the tests measure. (p. 564)

Even the DIBELS assessment of accuracy is suspect. Children who skip several words are not penalized at all since the score is the number of words read *correctly* in one minute with no reduction in score for words missed, however many there are. Thus, the test ends up being a measure of reading rate only.

An assessment such as the DIBELS is quick and easy to administer and score, but it does not validly assess fluency; it assesses children based only on whether they are fast readers and suggests practice activities to help them read faster and thus improve their test performance. Consequently, fluency—the important ability to read words in connected text accurately, quickly, with appropriate phrasing and expression, and comprehension—goes untested and untaught.

Another way assessment can hinder rather than promote good instruction is a direct result of the goals of NCLB: all students reading on grade level. Consider what this goal really means: grade level is average. The way test makers determine how many items students must answer correctly for a grade-level score is to take all the scores and divide by the number of students who took the test. Some students will score below the average score, and some will score above it. It is mathematically impossible for everyone to be average, and yet that was the goal set for teachers under NCLB. Trying to meet that goal had disastrous consequences for teachers and students, especially for those in schools with high numbers of students from low socioeconomic backgrounds. A cheating scandal, such as the one in Atlanta in which forty-four schools were found to have erased and changed children's incorrect answers on high-stakes tests, is inexcusable but probably inevitable when a goal is set that cannot be met. The assessments mandated by NCLB were impossible to meet, and attempts to meet them hindered good instruction by taking valuable time from instruction. In addition, teachers in schools with a high population of students from low socioeconomic backgrounds may come to resent the children they are teaching.

Trust between teachers, students, and parents has been shown to play a key role in enhancing student achievement in urban elementary schools (Bryk & Schneider, 2002; Goddard, Tschannen-Moran, & Hoy, 2001). This trusting relationship between teachers and their students is eroded when teachers see their students as keeping them from meeting their goals, endangering their jobs and the job of their principal.

If done correctly, reading assessment can help rather than hinder learning. The emphasis on assessment is now shifting to focus more on the progress that students make, rather than enforcing a single grade-level standard for all:

> By all accounts and appearances, accountability for achievement gains for disaggregated groups will remain, with more flexibility provided to capture growth; more and more states will be allowed to use growth models rather than counting the number of students achieving a particular performance standard. (Foorman & Connor, 2011, p. 150)

Assessment promotes good instruction when the assessments schools use validly measure what educators want them to measure, when teachers use the results of those assessments to help make good instructional decisions, and when progress—rather than a single grade-level standard—is the goal that both students and educators can embrace and work toward.

The School Schedule Affects Literacy Instruction

One of the most difficult tasks of an administrator is making the master schedule for the school. Teachers often don't want specials classes (such as music, art, and physical education) first thing in the morning. Everyone wants to go to the playground in the late afternoon. Specialists want to work with children with similar needs together at the same time. These are valid desires; however, it's unlikely—if not impossible—for administrators to please everyone, so principals must approach the task of creating the master schedule with benefits to both students and teachers in mind.

To make the most of literacy instruction, we recommend that the master schedule give priority to blocks of uninterrupted time for literacy instruction—at least 120 minutes in the primary grades and 90 minutes in the upper grades (Allington & Cunningham, 2007). For primary students, it is important that this uninterrupted time be before lunch because many young children are much more able to engage in academic work in the mornings. Older students need uninterrupted time as well, but that time can, if necessary, be scheduled in the afternoon. The time must be truly uninterrupted—students should not be pulled out for special instruction, parents should not be allowed to drop in on the classrooms, and only in true emergencies should the intercom or telephone interrupt instruction.

This uninterrupted block of time allows teachers to provide quality instruction in all the different components of literacy. Teachers will have time to work with the whole class, small groups, and individuals using whatever format they feel is most effective for the goals they seek to accomplish. Teachers will have time to read aloud to students, and students can do writing that connects with what they are reading. In addition to getting reading instruction from the teacher, students will have time for independent reading and working collaboratively with others.

Perhaps as important, providing teachers with uninterrupted time to teach reading sends a powerful message that school leaders believe that every child learning to read well is important, that reading is a complex subject to teach, and that good reading instruction takes time.

Building Your Reading Program

This chapter has summarized six overriding ideas that underpin good instruction in all areas of reading. The next eight chapters of this book will address the individual components of a comprehensive and effective reading program. When thinking about the components presented in the next chapters, keep the six ideas in mind:

1. Reading is complex.
2. Reading First didn't work.
3. All schools can increase reading achievement.
4. Effective literacy instruction requires a supportive, nurturing classroom environment.
5. Assessment can promote or hinder good instruction.
6. The school schedule affects literacy instruction.

TWO
COMPREHENSION

Comprehension—thinking about and responding to what one is reading—is the prime reason for engaging in reading. The questions surrounding comprehension—what it is, how it occurs, and how it should be taught—have driven hundreds of research studies since the 1970s. Reading comprehension and how to teach it is probably the area of literacy about which we have the most knowledge and have achieved the most consensus. Unfortunately, it is an area that gets little attention in the classroom. If researchers and educators agree that comprehension is what reading is all about, then why isn't it taught more often?

The Roadblocks to Comprehension

We believe there are three roadblocks that keep teachers from teaching comprehension, and that these roadblocks keep many students from becoming thoughtful, responsive readers. Some of the roadblocks reflect misconceptions or belief systems that lead to inadequate, ineffective, or inappropriate instruction.

The Belief That Assessing Comprehension Teaches Comprehension

In 1979, Dolores Durkin published a landmark study demonstrating that little, if any, reading comprehension *instruction* happens in most classrooms. What she observed instead was teachers *assessing* comprehension, primarily by asking individual students to answer oral or written comprehension questions. This finding has been replicated in other studies since then (Beck, McKeown, & Gromoll, 1989; Pressley & Wharton-McDonald, 1998), and no studies have refuted it. In our experience, having students answer comprehension questions orally or in writing remains the most common reading comprehension activity in classrooms.

We offer the following analogy to shed light on how comprehension is taught in most classrooms: Imagine that your blood pressure is high. Your doctor will probably recommend a change in diet, more exercise, and losing a few pounds. If your blood pressure is still high after adopting these healthier habits, your doctor will probably prescribe medication. Comprehension questions are like blood-pressure checks: they assess the current situation—a student's understanding. The doctor's interventions—a change in diet, increased exercise, losing weight, and medication—are like comprehension instruction. Just as checking your blood pressure regularly will not lower your blood pressure, answering comprehension questions without comprehension instruction will not teach students how to comprehend better.

The Belief That Comprehension "Just Happens"

As adults, we comprehend most of what we read automatically and effortlessly; it's little wonder we think comprehension is automatic. For students, however, comprehension does not necessarily happen automatically, regardless of how well they understand individual words. What would keep a student from comprehending something if he or she could read almost all the words and knew the word meanings? Answering that question involves consideration of what comprehension is.

Comprehension is essentially thinking—but what is thinking? In 1956, Benjamin Bloom and other educational psychologists developed a classification of levels of intellectual behavior important in learning (Bloom, Engelhart, Furst, Hill, & Krathwohl, 1956). Bloom's Taxonomy has long been viewed as defining what we commonly call *thinking*. His original taxonomy had six levels: evaluation, synthesis, analysis, application, comprehension, and knowledge. During the late 1990s, a new group of cognitive psychologists led by Lorin Anderson (a former student of Bloom's), updated the levels of the taxonomy to: creating, evaluating, analyzing, applying, understanding, and remembering (Anderson et al., 2001).

The power and usefulness of Bloom's Taxonomy have been to help teachers understand that when teaching any area of the curriculum, it is necessary and beneficial to teach students how to do each kind of thinking (creating, evaluating, analyzing, applying, understanding, and remembering). The same is true in reading. Just because a student can identify the words in a text and knows the appropriate meanings still does not mean the student is able to do each kind of thinking while reading the text. Adequate word identification and vocabulary instruction are not enough to make students good comprehenders. They must also receive comprehension instruction so they can learn how to create, evaluate, analyze, apply, understand, and remember—especially as they encounter increasingly difficult materials.

Bloom's Taxonomy also helps educators understand how instruction can differ when teaching students to think about what they read. If teachers are focusing on the lower levels of thinking—remembering and understanding—they can require students to recall or explain what they have read. Moving up to the next level of thinking—applying—teachers might ask students to dramatize what they read or to illustrate a portion of it. If teachers want the students to analyze, they can ask the students to compare and contrast two or more events in the text. The highest levels of thinking require students to evaluate (to give their opinions and support them with facts) and to create (to construct something new based on what they read). The combination of tasks that develop comprehension and emphasis on higher-level thinking makes reading comprehension lessons more interesting and successful for both teachers and students.

The research demonstrates that comprehension can indeed be taught. For example, in a large study that included eighty-eight teachers in nine high-poverty schools, teachers who emphasized higher-order thinking achieved the greatest reading growth (Taylor, Pearson, Peterson, & Rodriguez, 2003). In 2010, the What Works Clearinghouse published its findings for what works in reading comprehension (Shanahan et al., 2010). Researchers reviewed all the experimental research on reading comprehension and made the following recommendations to improve reading comprehension:

- Teach students to use reading comprehension strategies (questioning, inferring, monitoring, and others).

- Teach students to identify and use the text's organizational structure (narrative and informational).

- Guide students through focused high-quality discussion on the meaning of text.

- Select texts purposefully to support comprehension development.

- Establish an engaging and motivating context in which to teach reading.

Comprehension doesn't just happen. These research-based recommendations provide means by which we can teach comprehension as thinking and emphasize higher-order thinking with all our students.

The Belief That Comprehension Can Wait

Many primary teachers fail to help their students learn to comprehend because all their teaching time and energy are allocated to the other components of reading: phonics, oral reading fluency, and meaning vocabulary. While it is understandable that word-level skills will be the focus of beginning reading instruction, there is danger in delaying comprehension instruction until the word-level skills are in place. Some students will expend so much of their energy on figuring out the words and reading them quickly that they won't be thinking about what they read. These students are known as "word callers"—their oral reading is proficient, but they can't tell the teacher much about what they've read. It is not surprising that more and more students are reading words and not thinking about what they are reading. Since the implementation of Reading First, the assessments in early grades have consisted mainly of words correct per minute on measures and phonics tests in which children read lists of nonsense words. By the time these children reach third or fourth grade, the "reading but not thinking" habit can be so automatic and ingrained that students are unable to read words and think about the meaning of those words simultaneously.

Word skills must be taught well to beginning readers; anyone who has taught beginners to read knows that you have to teach them to rapidly identify sight words, to decode less common words, and to know meanings for important but unfamiliar words. However, comprehension cannot be allowed to wait its turn. From the very beginning, students should have a purpose for reading that requires them not only to say the words but to think about what those words together are telling them.

As we will demonstrate later in chapter 5 on phonics, research refutes the belief that all students who struggle in reading beyond the primary grades lack phonics skills. Some do, but most do not. In K–2, also, many struggling readers fail to receive the comprehension instruction they need because almost all the instructional time is taken up by phonics and fluency.

Comprehension and the Common Core Standards

Asking comprehension questions is not the same as teaching comprehension; comprehension can be taught, and it needs to be taught from the very beginning of reading instruction. The recent adoption of the Common Core State Standards (CCSS) by almost all states in the United States has expanded the view of comprehension, and it has become the focus of reading standards.

The CCSS include standards for both reading instruction and reading across the curriculum, with standards relating to informational texts as well as literature at every grade from K through 12. They consist of ten anchor reading standards applied across the grades, for both types of text (informational and literature), and in curricular subjects. Six of the first nine anchor standards address different kinds of reading comprehension (1, 2, 3, 4, 8, and 9) while the last (10) specifies the text difficulty at which students at each grade should be able to meet the first nine standards. An examination of the reading standards at any grade will quickly reveal that the CCSS have significantly raised reading comprehension expectations for everyone in every subject. For example, consider the following reading standards from grade 2 (National Governors Association Center for Best Practices & Council of Chief State School Officers, 2010, pp. 11, 13):

- Ask and answer such questions as *who, what, where, when, why,* and *how* to demonstrate understanding of key details in a text. (RL.2.1)

- Compare and contrast two or more versions of the same story (such as Cinderella stories) by different authors or from different cultures. (RL.2.9)

- Describe the connection between a series of historical events, scientific ideas or ·concepts, or steps in technical procedures in a text. (RI.2.3)

Comprehension, including higher-level thinking, is the major goal of the CCSS in reading. It is difficult to imagine that most second graders could meet the standards noted previously without a strong and continuing emphasis on comprehension from the very beginning of reading instruction.

As students progress through the grades, the reading standards require higher-level thinking skills almost exclusively as shown in the following grade 5 standards (NGA & CCSSO, 2010, p. 12):

- Describe how a narrator's or speaker's point of view influences how events are described. (RL.5.6)

- Analyze multiple accounts of the same event or topic, noting important similarities and differences in the point of view they represent. (RI.5.6)

- Integrate information from several texts on the same topic in order to write or speak about the subject knowledgeably. (RI.5.9)

The reading standards for grade 8 would challenge the analysis and application skills of many educated adults. Consider the following examples (NGA & CCSSO, 2010, pp. 39, 44):

- Delineate and evaluate the argument and specific claims in a text, assessing whether the reasoning is sound and the evidence is relevant and sufficient; recognize when irrelevant evidence is introduced. (RI.8.8)

- Analyze a case in which two or more texts provide conflicting information on the same topic and identify where the texts disagree on matters of fact or interpretation. (RI.8.9)

- Analyze how a modern work of fiction draws on themes, patterns of events, or character types from myths, traditional stories, or religious works such as the Bible, including describing how the material is rendered new. (RL.8.9)

The CCSS have significantly raised the requirements for reading proficiency. Our students are going to have to demonstrate levels and kinds of comprehension that go far beyond what was previously considered adequate.

Best Practices for Comprehension Instruction

Once you know what to look for—both the roadblocks and best practices—you can determine the state of comprehension instruction in your school. Here are some best practices in comprehension instruction.

Teachers Emphasize Students Thinking About What They Read

Teachers who are effective in reading instruction infuse comprehension into every reading lesson. This is considered best practice in grades 3 and above, but is also true even with beginning readers. Primary teachers can promote comprehension in simple ways while reading aloud to students, when students are reading in small groups, and when students are reading independently, such as the following:

- When reading a story, ask students to choose their favorite part. Then ask several students to find the page that contained their favorite part and tell why that was their favorite part.

- When reading informational books, ask students to decide what was the most interesting new fact they learned. Then ask students to find the page and share their fact.

- After reading a story with pictures, ask students to retell the story by paging through the book and using the pictures to tell what happened on each page.

- When reading an informational book with pictures, ask students to page through the book and tell what they learned on each page.

- For books with few pictures, ask students to choose their favorite part (of a story) or the most interesting fact (for informational books) and draw something to illustrate that part.

- Tell students that sometimes they will read something and not be able to figure out what it means. Give each student two or three sticky notes, asking them to draw a huge question mark on each note. As they read, they should place the sticky notes right on the places in the text that confused them. This is a concrete way to remind students that when they are reading, they have to think about what they are reading. (An added plus is that students love sticky notes and drawing big question marks.)

Teachers Set Clear Purposes and Follow Them Up

When good readers read, they have a purpose in mind. Although we are often unaware of that purpose, it guides our thinking. The purpose tells us what details we need to pay attention to and which we can ignore. For example, when reading a mystery, we attempt to figure out "who done it" by looking for clues in the text. Reading a review of different models of cars in *Consumer Reports* involves looking for specific details—perhaps about mileage and safety, for example—and comparing and contrasting different models and brands. When reading a magazine article on South Africa, we might consider which places would be fun to visit.

When we read, we can't possibly pay attention to everything. Having a purpose for reading focuses our brain on the details and ideas that help us achieve that purpose. Giving students a clear purpose for reading and following up on that purpose after students read is one simple practice teachers can integrate into their reading lessons. For example, asking students to read a text with a mundane title to think of a better one helps them focus simultaneously on overall meaning, theme, and style, rather than getting bogged down in details. For another example, having students read so they can construct a web of the content focuses their attention on the subtopical organization of the text. This research-supported strategy (Ramsay & Sperling, 2010), if used regularly, helps students to become more mature readers.

Teachers Set Purposes That Require Higher-Level Thinking

The two lowest levels of Bloom's Taxonomy—understanding and remembering—mainly require literal comprehension of each sentence. Most of the thinking the brain does when reading, however, moves beyond the literal and sentence levels. For example, we analyze the events in a mystery as we try to figure out who did it. We apply what we read in a review of different cars so we can make an educated decision about which car to purchase. We evaluate the possible destinations in South Africa and decide which sites to see.

Some teachers believe students cannot do higher-level thinking; this is simply not true. In fact, some of the students most at risk for reading failure face situations every day outside of school that require them to analyze, apply, evaluate, and create as they solve problems and avoid dangerous situations. Almost all students participate in higher-level thinking outside of school, but when they read, they often read with a mindset to simply "get the facts." Perhaps that is because so many of the questions teachers ask after reading are low-level factual questions that test whether or not students read—as if comprehension was a discipline rather than instructional problem. All students must engage in higher-level thinking to be successful in life.

When mature readers think about what they are reading, they pay attention to the facts and details, but only in order to use those facts and details to build bigger ideas. This higher-level comprehension is what is referred to as *inferential comprehension* and *critical reading.*

Shanahan and colleagues' research synthesis (2010) identifies six thinking strategies found to positively affect reading comprehension:

1. Using prior knowledge and predicting

2. Questioning

3. Visualizing

4. Monitoring

5. Drawing inferences

6. Retelling and summarizing

All six of these strategies require some kind of higher-level thinking, including retelling when it is accompanied by summarizing. Teachers help students improve their reading comprehension over time when they set purposes for reading and follow up those purposes with comprehension tasks that require students to move to higher levels of thinking and help them when they have difficulty. When students read knowing they will write about or discuss the text afterwards, it leads them to consider the significant ideas much more than when they know they will be asked merely to retell or answer detail questions.

Teachers Model How to Think About Reading

Imagine you have a friend who is a gourmet cook. She invites you for dinner one night and serves incredible ravioli. You comment on how extraordinary the ravioli is and ask her what brand it is. She laughs and says, "Oh, I didn't buy the ravioli. I made it!" You decide you also want to learn to make ravioli from scratch. You set a date, and a few weeks later, you and she make ravioli together. She models each step and then watches while you take over, giving you pointers along the way. A few weeks later, you astound some other friends with your ravioli. (They want to know what brand it is too!)

In real life, if we are teaching someone to do something, we don't just tell him or her what to do—we also show what to do. In teaching, we call this *modeling.* Teachers can use think-alouds to model how their brain thinks as they read aloud. These think-alouds during read-alouds (see Keene & Zimmerman, 2007) are a way for teachers to model or make public the thinking they do as they read. The teacher shows students how the brain accesses prior knowledge by stopping during his or her reading to make comments such as the following:

- "This reminds me of . . ."
- "I read another book where the character . . ."
- "This is like in our school when . . ."
- "Our country doesn't have that holiday, but we have . . ."

Think-alouds that model asking questions and making predictions usually begin with words such as the following:

- "I wonder if . . ."
- "I wonder who . . ."
- "I think I know what is coming next . . ."
- "He will be in trouble if . . ."
- "I think I will learn that . . ."

Periodically, the teacher stops during reading and summarizes what has happened or what he or she has learned with phrases such as:

- "The most important thing I've learned so far is . . ."
- "So far in the story . . ."

Then, the teacher analyzes what he or she is reading, makes inferences, and draws conclusions, modeling them in this way:

- "It didn't say why she did that, but I bet . . ."
- "I know he must be feeling . . ."

The teacher can model how his or her brain visualizes and creates images and pictures by interrupting the reading with statements such as the following:

- "Even though it isn't in the picture, I can see the . . ."
- "That sent chills down my spine when it said . . ."
- "I can imagine what it is like to . . ."
- "I can picture the . . ."

The brain also makes evaluations and judgments and monitors how well one comprehends what is being learned. To show this, teachers can make statements such as:

- "I wonder what it means when it says . . ."

- "It didn't make sense when . . ."

- "I really liked how the author . . ."

- "It was really interesting to learn that . . ."

- "I am going to try this out when I . . ."

- "If I were her, I would . . ."

Thinking aloud when reading aloud is the most direct way to teach students how the brain thinks during reading. Teachers who include think-aloud modeling as part of their reading instruction take the opportunity to show—rather than just tell—their students how good readers understand what they read.

Teachers Focus Discussions on Higher-Level Thinking

Teachers modeling how the brain thinks during reading is the most direct way to show students how to think as they read. For example, if students are going to read an informational text about Brazil from a children's magazine or newspaper, such as *TIME For Kids* or *Weekly Reader*, the teacher could give them a fairly low-level purpose of understanding and remembering, such as "Read the article about Brazil so that we can talk about what life is like in Brazil." Or the teacher could require higher-level analyzing by telling students, "After you read the article, we are going to compare and contrast what life is like in Brazil and in our country." Discussions should then move students to the higher levels of applying and evaluating. For example:

> You are going to read about Brazil. You will discover many similarities and some differences about how children your age live in Brazil. I want you to use your imaginations as you read and pretend that you and your family move to Brazil. What things would be just like they are in this country? What things would be different? What would you like better about life in Brazil? What would you miss about the way we do things in the United States? After you read, we will talk about how Brazil and our country are the same and different and what you would like better there or here.

Sometimes teachers have difficulty getting students to engage in discussions. Often that is because students are used to reading for low-level facts where there is little to discuss. When teachers set a purpose for discussion that engages students in higher-level thinking, students gradually become more ready to share their opinions. Of course, to form those opinions, students have to pay attention to the relevant facts and details, but they do not become fixated on memorization of those facts.

Teachers Gradually Release Responsibility for Comprehension to Students

The gradual-release-of-responsibility model of instruction (Pearson & Gallagher, 1983) suggests that in order for students to learn to do something, instruction in that skill or strategy must shift from the teacher to the student. There are various ways to conceptualize how this shift might occur in the classroom. Many teachers remind themselves of the need to move students toward independence by thinking about their instruction like this:

> I do the task, you watch. ➔ I do the task, you help. ➔ You do the task, I help. ➔ You do the task, I watch.

Other teachers move from teacher modeling and guidance to collaborative group implementation and finally to independence in the following way:

> I do the task, you watch. ➔ We do the task together. ➔ You do the task together. ➔ You do the task alone.

To be effective, comprehension instruction must begin with some kind of scaffolding, and gradually that scaffolding must be removed. As you observe teachers delivering comprehension instruction, think about where the instruction lies on the continuum to student independence. Look at lesson plans across time to determine how aware teachers are of the need both to provide modeling and instruction and to move students to independence with what they've been modeling and teaching.

Students Read Narrative *and* Informational Text

Many students who have been pretty good readers in the early grades suddenly develop comprehension problems in the intermediate grades. These students are often fluent readers with adequate meaning vocabularies and may even be avid readers of stories. Reading stories, however, is very different from reading informational text (Duke, 2010). One of the five recommendations from the What Works Clearinghouse research synthesis (Shanahan et al., 2010) is to teach students to comprehend both narrative and informational texts. The CCSS include reading standards for informational texts at every grade from K through 12. The current NAEP Reading test includes informational texts; assessments for the CCSS are expected to include many informational texts.

Teaching students to comprehend the informational texts they encounter in science and social studies is so important that chapter 4 of this book is devoted to the topic.

Resources for Comprehension Study Groups

If improving comprehension instruction in your school is one of your priorities, see the reproducible list of resources on page 28. These resources provide detailed descriptions and lesson templates that will help your teachers overcome the roadblocks and implement the best practices described in this chapter. Articles from *The Reading Teacher* are included because they are quick reads that can launch your discussions and because they are accessible online with a subscription.

The State of Comprehension Instruction in Your School

This chapter has answered three important questions about comprehension: What misconceptions act as roadblocks in the way of implementing better comprehension instruction? What does good comprehension instruction look like? What specific resources could you use to help your teachers improve their comprehension instruction?

Compared with other areas of reading, comprehension instruction may be a relative weakness or strength in your school. To help you decide whether you need to intervene with some or all of your teachers with a study group or other professional development, we have compiled an informal checklist (page 29) for considering the state of comprehension instruction in your school. If you decide an intervention is needed in comprehension instruction, you may find the same checklist useful to help you determine the effectiveness of the intervention.

Comprehension Resources

This document summarizes the research on reading comprehension and recommends practical teaching strategies for implementing the seven research-based best practices outlined in chapter 2:

- Shanahan, T., Callison, K., Carriere, C., Duke, N. K., Pearson, P. D., Schatschneider, C., et al. (2010). *Improving reading comprehension in kindergarten through 3rd grade: A practice guide* (NCEE 2010-4038). Washington, DC: National Center for Education Evaluation and Regional Assistance, Institute of Education Sciences, U.S. Department of Education. Accessed at http://ies.ed.gov/ncee/wwc/pdf/practiceguides/readingcomp _pg_092810.pdf on March 13, 2012.

This is a valuable resource for think-alouds that is full of examples and tips for successful modeling of higher-level thinking:

- Keene, E. O., & Zimmerman, S. (2007). *Mosaic of thought: The power of comprehension strategy instruction* (2nd ed.). Portsmouth, NH: Heinemann.

The following books contain examples for lesson formats to teach reading strategies for both narrative and informational text:

- Cunningham, P. W., Hall, D. P., & Cunningham, J. W. (2011). *Comprehension during guided, shared and independent reading, grades K–6*. Greensboro, NC: Carson-Dellosa.

- Fisher, D., Frey, N., & Lapp, D. (2012). *Teaching students to read like detectives: Comprehending, analyzing, and discussing text*. Bloomington, IN: Solution Tree Press

- Harvey, S., & Goudvis, A. (2007). *Strategies that work: Teaching comprehension for understanding and engagement* (2nd ed.). Portland, ME: Stenhouse.

- Miller, D. (2002). *Reading with meaning: Teaching comprehension in the primary grades*. Portland, ME: Stenhouse.

- Taberski, S. (2011). *Comprehension from the ground up: Simplified, sensible instruction for K–3 workshop reading*. Portsmouth, NH: Heinemann.

The following book provides examples of lessons that move students to higher levels of thinking when they are reading stories:

- Cunningham, P. W., & Smith, D. R. (2008). *Beyond retelling: Toward higher-level thinking and big ideas*. Boston: Pearson.

In addition to many suggestions for teaching strategies, these two books describe how teachers can gradually shift responsibility for comprehension to students and move them toward independence:

- Fisher, D., & Frey, N. (2008). *Better learning through structured teaching: A framework for the gradual release of responsibility*. Alexandria, VA: Association for Supervision and Curriculum Development.

- Wilhelm, J. (2004). *Reading is seeing: Learning to visualize scenes, characters, ideas, and text worlds to improve comprehension and reflective reading*. New York: Scholastic.

The following are very practical articles on comprehension from *The Reading Teacher* (www.reading.org /General/Publications/Journals/RT.aspx):

- Stricklin, K. (2011). Hands-on reciprocal teaching: A comprehension technique. *The Reading Teacher, 64*(8), 620–625.

- Talking about books to improve comprehension. (2010). *The Reading Teacher, 64*(1), 77–80.

Comprehension Instruction: What to Look For

As you observe in classrooms and examine lesson plans and class schedules, ask the following questions about what you see, hear, and read:

1. Do all teachers emphasize comprehension, even with beginning readers?

   ☐ Frequently   ☐ Occasionally   ☐ Rarely   ☐ Never

   Comments:

2. Do teachers set clear purposes for reading and follow them up after reading?

   ☐ Frequently   ☐ Occasionally   ☐ Rarely   ☐ Never

   Comments:

3. Do the purposes teachers set for reading require higher-level thinking?

   ☐ Frequently   ☐ Occasionally   ☐ Rarely   ☐ Never

   Comments:

4. Do teachers model for students how to think about reading?

   ☐ Frequently   ☐ Occasionally   ☐ Rarely   ☐ Never

   Comments:

5. Do teachers focus discussions after reading on higher-level thinking?

   ☐ Frequently   ☐ Occasionally   ☐ Rarely   ☐ Never

   Comments:

6. Do teachers gradually release responsibility for comprehension to students?

   ☐ Frequently   ☐ Occasionally   ☐ Rarely   ☐ Never

   Comments:

7. Do teachers have students read both narrative and informational text?

   ☐ Frequently   ☐ Occasionally   ☐ Rarely   ☐ Never

   Comments:

THREE

VOCABULARY

How many words do you know—5,000? 10,000? 20,000? 50,000? 100,000? This might seem like a straightforward question, though certainly difficult to answer. It brings up the question, What exactly does it mean to *know* a word? Is it enough to know, for example, that *anthropoids* are a kind of ape, or does one have to know that anthropoids are apes without tails, such as chimpanzees, gorillas, orangutans, and gibbons? This leads to the next question: how many meanings of the word must we know? For example, if one knows what a *coach* is on a sports team, does one also need to know what *coach* means in relation to a bus or airplane to count the word as known? What about the various forms of a single word: *play, plays, playing, played, playful, replay,* and *player*?

Biemiller (2004) estimates that students entering kindergarten have meanings for an average of 3,500 root words. Children add approximately 1,000 root word meanings each school year. The average high school graduate knows about 15,000 root words. Other vocabulary experts (Graves, 2006; Stahl & Nagy, 2006) argue that Biemiller's estimate is way too low. They believe that words with multiple meanings should be counted as separate words and that many children do not recognize words with common roots. Furthermore, they believe that proper nouns—Canada, Abraham Lincoln, London, the White House—should be included in the total word count. When counted in this way, the average child learns 2,000 to 3,000 word meanings each school year, and the average high school graduate has meanings for 40,000 to 50,000 words. Regardless of which estimates you believe, the number of new words children need to add to their vocabularies each year is staggering.

Children differ greatly, however, in the sizes of their meaning vocabularies at school entrance and as they continue through the grades. Children who enter school with small vocabularies tend to add fewer words each year than children who enter with larger vocabularies. Since vocabulary size is so closely related to comprehension as students move through school, there is a sense of urgency about intensifying efforts to build larger and deeper word meaning stores for all children.

The Roadblocks to Vocabulary Instruction

Everyone knows that vocabulary matters; words are the tools we use to understand when we read and communicate our ideas when we write. Building new word meanings, however, is neither simple nor quick. We believe there are three common roadblocks to effective vocabulary instruction in most classrooms.

The Belief That Vocabulary Instruction Is "Learning Definitions"

Read the following three words, and think about what comes immediately to your mind: *plastic, purple, racket*. What did you think of for the word *plastic*? Did you imagine all the plastic objects that make up everyday life? Did you experience negative feelings, such as "I hate using plastic knives, forks, and spoons," while simultaneously realizing that our current world would be very different if it weren't for the omnipresence of plastic? Did you worry because plastic biodegrades so slowly and is not good for the environment? Did you recall one of the most famous lines in movie history from *The Graduate*?

What did your brain do with the word *purple*? Did you picture something purple? Did you think "I hate purple" or "Purple is my favorite color"? Did you imagine different shades of purple—orchid, lavender, lilac? Perhaps the word *purple* made you think immediately of someone you know who was in the military and earned a Purple Heart.

Did you picture a tennis or badminton racket for the word *racket*? Or did you think of the racket being made by the construction across the street? Perhaps you were reminded about the shenanigans of your local government and thought, "It's all a racket!"

When we see or hear words, our brains make all kinds of connections with those words, depending on our past experiences. These connections include images and scenes from our own lives as well as from movies and television. We have emotional reactions to words. Words make us worry, celebrate, appreciate, and wonder.

What our minds don't do when we see or hear a word is think of a definition. Look up *plastic*, *purple*, and *racket* in a dictionary, and you will find definitions such as these:

- Plastic—any of a large group of synthetic organic compounds molded by heat pressure into a variety of forms

- Purple—a color made by mixing red and blue

- Racket—a loud noise; a scheme for getting money illegally; an oval, strung frame with a long handle used for hitting balls

Now think back to your school days and recall your associations with the word *vocabulary*. Do you remember looking up words and copying their definitions? If a word had several definitions, did you copy the first one or the shortest one? Did you ever look up a word and still not know what it meant because you did not understand the meanings of the other words in the definition? Did you copy that definition and memorize it for the test, in spite of not understanding it? Do you remember weekly vocabulary tests for which you had to write definitions for words and use those words in sentences?

Copying and memorizing definitions remains the most common vocabulary activity in schools. It is done at all levels and in all subjects. In a major review of research on vocabulary instruction, copying and memorizing definitions was shown to increase students' ability to define words but has no positive effect on writing or reading comprehension (Baumann, Kame'enui, & Ash, 2003).

Teachers Overwhelmed by the Size of the Task

Students should be adding from 1,000 to 3,000 new words to their meaning vocabulary stores each year. For example, if the number of new words students need to add each school year is 1,800, dividing that number by the average number of school days means that teachers must teach ten new word meanings every day—that's fifty every single week! Teaching that many new word meanings is impossible, and teachers realize it. Teaching a new word meaning is not as simple as introducing the word. Word meanings grow like onions—the first encounter with a new word is the tiny bulb of the onion. Each time we encounter and use that word, we add layers of meaning. If teachers introduce a new word to students, students must use it, review it, and add to its meaning across several days.

Teaching 1,000 to 3,000 new word meanings every year of school cannot possibly be done, and yet students on average gain that many new word meanings a year. How can this be? Vocabulary experts agree that while some new word meanings are directly taught, students acquire many through reading. When students come across a word in their reading, they have two sources of information to help them figure out the meaning of that word: context and morphology.

Consider the following sentence: I wish I understood how they colorize old movies. If you had never heard the word *colorize* before, you probably figured out what it meant by using the context of the sentence and your morphemic knowledge about the root *color* and the suffix *ize*. Since you know that when you *modernize* something, you make it more modern and when you *rationalize* something you have done, you make it rational, you quickly realize that to *colorize* something is to make it have color.

Most of the words we have in our meaning vocabulary stores that we didn't have when we entered school we have learned from reading by using context and our implicit understanding of roots, prefixes, and suffixes. To promote vocabulary growth in all students, teachers must directly teach word meanings for unknown words that all students need to learn, ensure students are engaging in a lot of reading, and teach them how to use context and morphology (knowledge of morphemes such as roots, prefixes, and suffixes) to determine meanings for unfamiliar words.

The Difficulty of Assessing Vocabulary Growth

Albert Einstein captured the essence of the dilemma schools face with assessment when he said, "Not everything that can be counted counts, and not everything that counts can be counted." Assessment has become a huge part of education these days, and, as described earlier, it can both promote and hinder good instruction. When teachers assess students' knowledge of the words they are directly teaching, teachers often resort to vocabulary tests in which students choose or write definitions. Yet word meanings are not stored in the brain by definition, and learning new definitions is not related to an increase in comprehension. How should teachers measure the vocabulary growth students are gaining through their reading, and how do teachers know how well students are using context and morphology to add new words to their vocabularies? In this area of accountability, not having valid short-term measures of vocabulary growth is a major roadblock to the effective teaching of meaning vocabulary.

The CCSS have significantly raised the expectations for reading proficiency; students now have to demonstrate comprehension skills that go way beyond the literal retellings and comprehension questions once considered adequate.

Strategies for acquiring new vocabulary and using vocabulary in all subject areas pervade the CCSS. The standards in the feature box on page 35 illustrate the sophisticated vocabulary strategies that fifth graders are expected to apply. Helping all students build large, deep, and precise vocabularies should be a major goal of all teachers because words are the building blocks for comprehension and communication. It is also pragmatic because students will not do well on Common Core assessments without rich vocabularies.

The State of Vocabulary Instruction in Your School

Once you know what to look for—both the roadblocks and best practices—you can determine the state of effective vocabulary instruction in your school. Here are some best practices in vocabulary instruction.

All Teachers Focus on Building Word Meanings

In the previous chapter, one of the roadblocks to effective comprehension instruction was the idea that comprehension had to wait its turn. Vocabulary instruction has a similar problem. In most schools, kindergarteners are assessed on their phonics and phonemic awareness knowledge, and first- and second-grade students are assessed in phonics and fluency. Children are promoted or retained, and teachers and schools are rewarded or punished, based on these assessments. Given this, it is not surprising that kindergarten and primary teachers spend little time and energy building meaning vocabulary. However, research and common sense demonstrate the shortsightedness of this narrow instructional focus.

In the study cited in chapter 1 (Juel et al., 2003) in which 200 low-income children were evaluated on their decoding and meaning vocabulary skills, students entering preschool showed deficits in both areas. The children improved in their decoding skills, but in vocabulary, they were as far behind in first grade as they had been in preschool. The researchers concluded that early literacy instruction for low-income children must emphasize both decoding and word meanings. Other research supports this conclusion. Researchers who measured the relationship between kindergarten meaning vocabulary and reading comprehension concluded that kindergarten vocabulary knowledge is a strong predictor of reading comprehension scores in third and fourth grades (Sénéchal, Ouellette, & Rodney, 2006).

Vocabulary and the Common Core State Standards

The Reading standard for grade 5 for Literature and Informative Text requires students to:

- Determine the meaning of words and phrases as they are used in a text, including figurative language such as metaphors and similes. (RL.5.4)
- Determine the meaning of general academic and domain-specific words and phrases in a text relevant to a grade 5 topic or subject area. (RI.5.4)

Language standards 4, 5, and 6 require fifth graders to be able to:

- Determine the meaning of unknown and multiple-meaning words and phrases based on grade 5 reading and content, choosing flexibly from a range of strategies. (L.5.4)
  - Use context as a clue to the meaning of a word or a phrase. (L.5.4a)
  - Use common, grade-appropriate Greek and Latin affixes and roots as a clue to the meaning of a word or phrase. (L.5.4b)
  - Consult reference materials, both print and digital, to find the pronunciation and determine or clarify the precise meaning of key words and phrases. (L.5.4c)
- Demonstrate understanding of figurative language, word relationships, and nuances in word meanings. (L.5.5)
  - Interpret figurative language including similes and metaphors in context. (L.5.5a)
  - Recognize and explain the meaning of common idioms, adages, and proverbs. (L.5.5b)
  - Use the relationship between particular words to better understand each of the words. (L.5.5c)
- Acquire and use accurately grade-appropriate general academic and domain-specific words and phrases, including those that signal contrast, addition, and other logical relationships. (L.5.6)

Source: NGA & CCSSO, 2010, pp. 12, 14, 29.

We know some of what effective vocabulary instruction in the elementary grades looks like. Prior to Reading First, vocabulary instruction occurred even in most kindergarten and primary classrooms as teachers taught units in science and social studies. Children learned meanings for words such as *habitats*, *shelter*, and *predators* as they learned about animals and the environment. They learned word meanings for *producers*, *consumers*, *goods*, and *services* as the teacher introduced basic economic concepts. These units, and the accompanying vocabulary development, disappeared from the curriculum in many schools, as almost all of the instructional time got allotted to the tested areas of phonics, phonemic awareness, and fluency. Decreasing the amount of vocabulary instruction was an unintended consequence of the shift in instructional emphasis in early grades. It is time to revisit the short-sighted decision to remove or drastically reduce time for science and social studies in the early grades.

Teachers Teach Important New Words

Teaching vocabulary should be a part of every reading lesson at every grade level. In addition to introducing new words and building meaning, teachers should make sure that students notice the new words as they encounter them in reading. After reading, students can volunteer to read aloud some sentences in which they found new words. They can then explain how these words were used and how reading them in context added to the depth of their meanings. Preteaching vocabulary is a common feature of most reading lessons. If pretaught words are ignored in the reading after they've been introduced, it is unlikely that children who didn't already have meanings for these words will add the words to their meaning vocabulary store. When observing vocabulary instruction, look for more than just introduction of new words. To add new word meanings, students must pay attention to those words in the text and use the words in some fashion after reading.

Teachers Teach Students How to Figure Out Word Meanings

As the saying goes, "Give me a fish and I will eat for a day; teach me to fish, and I eat for a lifetime." When teachers teach students meanings for new words before reading, they give their students a fish. Some words need to be taught in this direct way. Other words, however, occur in a rich context, sometimes with pictures and morphology clues (roots, inflections, prefixes, and suffixes). Teachers teach students how to fish with instruction in using context and morphology to find the meanings of new words they encounter.

Teachers can do this by identifying two or three words that students do not have deep meanings for during every reading lesson but whose meanings could be determined by using text clues (including context, pictures, and morphology). Students might write these words on individual sticky notes. As they read and encounter these words, they place the sticky notes on the words and use whatever clues the text provides to figure out what they think the words mean. After reading, students explain what they think the words mean and what clues helped them. Students enjoy being "word detectives" and finding clues. This simple modification to the traditional vocabulary instruction of new words increases student engagement and motivation and teaches students how to use text clues for determining the meanings of unknown words they encounter.

Teachers Teach Important New Words in Math, Science, and Social Studies

As important as it is to focus on word meanings when teaching reading, it is even more critical that teachers focus on meaning vocabulary as they teach math, science, and social studies. Key words in these subject areas are called *academic vocabulary*, and the lack of academic vocabulary is a major stumbling block to reading comprehension as students progress through elementary, middle, and high school. Focusing on vocabulary and comprehension while teaching math, science, and social studies is so important that the next chapter is devoted to the topic.

Teacher Read-Alouds and Independent Reading Occur Daily

The best readers spend the most time reading and have the largest vocabularies. To increase the size of the meaning vocabularies of all students, teachers must teach some important words, teach students to use text clues to figure out word meanings, and provide motivation and time for students to develop the habit of reading. Teachers should schedule time each day for reading aloud to students and time for students to engage in independent reading with books of their choosing. Chapter 7 addresses this topic in more detail.

Teachers Demonstrate Enthusiasm for Words

The final element in effective vocabulary instruction is perhaps one of the most critical: the attitude of the teacher. Effective teachers demonstrate an enthusiasm for words and an attitude that words are wonderful. Their "word wonder" is contagious. Teachers who are fascinated with words transmit their enthusiasm to their students, whereas teachers who view teaching new word meanings as drudgery transmit that attitude to their students.

There are a variety of ways teachers can communicate a words-are-wonderful attitude to their students. Practical suggestions for developing word consciousness and word wonder can be found in the list of resources on page 39. The books by Hallie K. Yopp, Ruth H. Yopp, and Ashley Bishop (2011) and Pat Cunningham (2009) both have an entire chapter on this topic.

Best Practices for Vocabulary Instruction

To close achievement gaps and make high levels of literacy possible for all children, educators must focus on meaning vocabulary. In 1977, Becker identified lack of meaning vocabulary as a crucial factor underlying the failure of many economically disadvantaged students. In 1995, Hart and Risley described a relationship between growing up in poverty and having a restricted vocabulary. In 2001, Biemiller and Slonim cited evidence that lack of vocabulary is a key component underlying school failure for disadvantaged students. Research supports both the direct teaching of some words and the teaching of vocabulary learning strategies (Baumann et al., 2003; Blachowicz & Fisher, 2000; Graves & Watts-Taffe, 2002).

If improving vocabulary instruction in your school is one of your priorities, see the reproducible list of resources on page 39. These resources contain detailed descriptions and lesson templates that will help your teachers overcome the roadblocks and implement the best practices described in this chapter. Articles from *The Reading Teacher* are included because they are quick reads that can launch your discussions and because they are accessible online with a subscription.

The State of Vocabulary Instruction in Your School

This chapter has answered three important questions about vocabulary: What misconceptions act as roadblocks in the way of implementing better vocabulary instruction? What does good vocabulary instruction look like? What specific resources could you use to help your teachers improve their vocabulary instruction?

Compared with other areas of reading, vocabulary instruction may be a relative weakness or strength in your school. To help you decide whether you need to intervene with some or all of your teachers with a study group or other professional development, we have compiled an informal checklist (page 40) for considering the state of vocabulary instruction in your school. If you decide an intervention is needed in vocabulary instruction, you may find the same checklist useful to help you determine the effectiveness of the intervention.

Vocabulary Resources

These books all have practical activities for teaching vocabulary in all areas of the elementary curriculum:

- Beck, I. L., McKeown, M. G., & Kucan, L. (2002). *Bringing words to life: Robust vocabulary instruction.* New York: Guilford Press.

- Blachowics, C., & Fisher, P. J. (2010). *Teaching vocabulary in all classrooms* (4th ed.). Boston: Allyn & Bacon.

- Cunningham, P. M. (2009). *What really matters in vocabulary: Research-based practices across the curriculum.* Boston: Pearson.

- Graves, M. F. (2006). *The vocabulary book: Learning & instruction.* New York: Teachers College Press.

- Yopp, H. K., Yopp, R. H., & Bishop, A. (2009). *Vocabulary instruction for academic success.* Huntington Beach, CA: Shell Education.

This lively book is full of examples, most of which are from upper-elementary and middle-school classrooms:

- Scott, J. A., Skobel, B. J., & Wells, J. (2008). *The word-conscious classroom: Building the vocabulary readers and writers need.* New York: Scholastic.

The following are very practical articles on vocabulary instruction from *The Reading Teacher*:

- Baumann, J. F., Ware, D., & Edwards, E. C. (2007). "Bumping into spicy, tasty words that catch your tongue": A formative experiment on vocabulary instruction. *The Reading Teacher, 61*(2), 108–122.

- Dalton, B., & Grisham, D. (2011). eVoc Strategies: 10 ways to use technology to build vocabulary. *The Reading Teacher, 64*(5), 306–317.

- Donnelly, W. B., & Roe, C. J. (2010). Using sentence frames to develop academic vocabulary for English learners. *The Reading Teacher, 64*(2), 131–136.

- Kelley, J. G., Lesaux, N. K., Kieffer, M. J., & Faller, S. E. (2010). Effective academic vocabulary instruction in the urban middle school. *The Reading Teacher, 64*(1), 5–14.

- Kindle, K. J. (2000). Vocabulary development during read-alouds. *The Reading Teacher, 63*(3), 202–211.

- Labbo, L. D., Love, M. S., & Ryan, T. (2007). A vocabulary flood: Making words "sticky" with computer-response activities. *The Reading Teacher, 60*(6), 582–588.

- Lane, L. B., & Allen, S. A. (2010). The vocabulary-rich classroom: Modeling sophisticated word use to promote word consciousness and vocabulary growth. *The Reading Teacher, 63*(5), 362–370.

- Manyak, P. C. (2010). Vocabulary instruction for English learners: Lessons from MCVIP. *The Reading Teacher, 64*(2), 143–146.

- Santoro, L. E., Chard, D. J., Howard, L., & Baker, S. K. (2008). Making the "very" most of classroom read-alouds to promote comprehension and vocabulary. *The Reading Teacher, 61*(5), 396–408.

- Wasik, B. A. (2010). What teachers can do to promote preschoolers' vocabulary development: Strategies from an effective language and literacy professional development coaching model. *The Reading Teacher, 63*(8), 621–633.

Vocabulary Instruction: What to Look For

As you observe in classrooms and examine lesson plans and class schedules, ask the following questions about what you see, hear, and read:

1. Do all teachers, even in the early grades, focus on building word meanings?

   ☐ Frequently   ☐ Occasionally   ☐ Rarely   ☐ Never

   Comments:

2. Do teachers teach meanings for important new words students will encounter in their reading?

   ☐ Frequently   ☐ Occasionally   ☐ Rarely   ☐ Never

   Comments:

3. Do teachers teach students to use context and morphology to figure out word meanings?

   ☐ Frequently   ☐ Occasionally   ☐ Rarely   ☐ Never

   Comments:

4. Do teachers teach academic or technical vocabulary needed to learn math, science, and social studies?

   ☐ Frequently   ☐ Occasionally   ☐ Rarely   ☐ Never

   Comments:

5. Do teachers take time each day for read-aloud and independent reading?

   ☐ Frequently   ☐ Occasionally   ☐ Rarely   ☐ Never

   Comments:

6. Do teachers demonstrate enthusiasm for words?

   ☐ Frequently   ☐ Occasionally   ☐ Rarely   ☐ Never

   Comments:

FOUR

LITERACY IN THE CONTENT AREAS

Since Hal Herber published his seminal text *Teaching Reading in Content Areas* (1970), reading experts have been encouraging every teacher to be a teacher of reading. In many states, history, science, and math teachers are required to take a content-area reading course. Schools hold in-service workshops, and experts and administrators instruct subject-area teachers to do their part in helping all students develop high levels of literacy. However, in spite of decades of valiant efforts, few subject-area teachers include reading as part of their instruction. Since the mid-1990s, the emphasis has shifted from every teacher teaching reading to every teacher teaching the language tools students need to learn the content. Each discipline has its own specialized vocabulary. Students need to learn the meanings of the technical and academic terms specific to each subject area so that they can comprehend what they are reading, listening to, or viewing and communicate their ideas about that subject in speaking and writing.

The Roadblocks to Literacy in the Content Areas

While it seems obvious that students need to learn the specific language of and how to communicate in each discipline, there is little evidence that subject-area teachers are focusing on teaching that language or helping students learn how to comprehend and communicate in that discipline. In our experience, there are three major roadblocks to effective literacy instruction in content areas.

Subject Teachers Think Teaching Reading Is Someone Else's Job

An unintended outcome of the movement toward every teacher as a teacher of reading has been resistance from subject-area teachers who believe that teaching reading should not be part of their job. This resistance has been supported by math, science, and social studies professors of education methods courses who fear that an emphasis on reading will take time and energy away from teaching their subject. The pressures of assessment and mandates to meet adequate yearly progress have fueled this resistance as subject-area teachers feel that their jobs and reputations depend on how well their students score on tests of math, science, and history—not on how well they read. Yet an examination of the materials used to prepare the students for the tests, and the tests themselves, usually contain academic vocabulary and informational text that can prevent learning and prevent students from being able to show what they know. Students who are not capable readers and writers seldom score well on tests in any subject area. When every teacher focuses on the language skills of listening, speaking, reading, and writing as he or she teaches a specific subject, test scores will better reflect what students have learned, not how well they read.

Teachers Teach the Way They Were Taught

As young students, all teachers experienced thousands of hours of instruction—some of it state of the art and some not. When beginning teachers come into their classrooms, their memories of schooling come with them. This probably explains the common phenomenon of an elementary teacher doing a terrific reading lesson in the morning—introducing vocabulary, building prior knowledge, giving students purposes for reading, modeling and leading students in discussions that build higher-level thinking—and then resorting to round-robin reading with low-level recall questions when teaching social studies in the afternoon. Even teachers who teach all subjects tend not to transfer their acquired knowledge about how to help students read better when they are teaching other subjects, but instead allow their childhood memories to guide them.

Teachers Avoid Reading in Math, Science, and Social Studies

There is no need to teach students the specific vocabulary and language tools needed to read in a subject area if the teacher requires little or no reading in that subject area. Sometimes the lack of reading is justified by the instructional demands of the subject area. Math teachers might rely on manipulatives and models to help students build mathematical concepts. Science teachers might want students to spend their time doing hands-on activities rather than reading about science. Social studies teachers might use visuals, simulations, and models for teaching to have students learn historical, economic, political, and geographic concepts.

Additionally, teachers might not require much reading because in many cases, the adopted textbooks are too difficult for most of their students to read. Unfortunately, textbooks at all grade levels may soon become even more challenging. At every grade level, CCSS Reading standard 10 includes a text complexity standard. The text complexity standard applies to informational text and texts across the curriculum. Appendix A of the Common Core State Standards for English Language Arts requires students at every grade to be able to read more difficult text than in the past. Publishers of textbooks at all levels are being urged to raise the readability levels of their books (Coleman & Pimentel, 2012a, 2012b). Assessments for the CCSS will reflect these higher readability levels. The feature box on page 43 shows what fifth graders are expected to be able to do as they read in science, social studies, and other technical subjects (NGA & CCSSO, 2010).

Common Core State Standards Go Across the Curriculum

- Quote accurately from a text when explaining what the text says explicitly and when drawing inferences from the text. (RI.5.1)

- Determine two or more main ideas of a text and explain how they are supported by key details; summarize the text. (RI.5.2)

- Explain the relationships or interactions between two or more individuals, events, ideas, or concepts in a historical, scientific, or technical text based on specific information in the text. (RI.5.3)

- Determine the meaning of general academic and domain-specific words and phrases in a text relevant to a grade 5 topic or subject area. (RI.5.4)

- Compare and contrast the overall structure (for example, chronology, comparison, cause/effect, problem/solution) of events, ideas, concepts, or information in two or more texts. (RI.5.5)

- Analyze multiple accounts of the same event or topic, noting important similarities and differences in the point of view they represent. (RI.5.6)

- Draw on information from multiple print or digital sources, demonstrating the ability to locate an answer to a question quickly or to solve a problem efficiently. (RI.5.7)

- Explain how an author uses reasons and evidence to support particular points in a text, identifying which reasons and evidence support which point(s). (RI.5.8)

- Integrate information from several texts on the same topic in order to write or speak about the subject knowledgeably. (RI.5.9)

- By the end of the year, read and comprehend informational texts, including history/social studies, science, and technical texts, at the high end of the grades 4–5 text complexity band independently and proficiently. (RI.5.10)

Source: NGA & CCSSO, 2010, p. 14.

Best Practices for Content-Area Literacy Instruction

Fair warning must be given before you attempt to evaluate how well the teachers on your staff are facilitating the language skills of listening, speaking, reading, and writing to help their students learn subject-area content. Unless you have an unusual staff, you may not see a lot of positive language facilitation! Look for the following indicators that teachers are providing students with the language tools they need.

Teachers Teach Key Vocabulary in Every Subject

Even in a subject in which virtually no reading occurs, building the academic or technical vocabulary of that content area should be a major focus of instruction. Academic vocabulary includes specialized terms such as *quadrilateral*, *polyhedron*, and *hexagon* as well as multi-meaning words which have a general meaning and a subject-specific meaning such as *problem*, *solve*, and *root* (Marzano & Pickering, 2005). Recall that the goal is not for every teacher to be a teacher of reading; rather, the goal is for every teacher to teach students to use language better to communicate—and words are the chief component of language.

Imagine you are visiting a classroom in which the teacher has set up a simulation to help students understand how economies work. Each student has a "job" and gets "paid" for doing a service or producing something. Students apply for the jobs they want and are interviewed about their skills and experience. They use the money they earn to pay rent for their desks and taxes for classroom services. The academic vocabulary these students would have hands-on experiences with would probably include the words *interview, skills, application, experience, economy, goods, services, producer, product, consumer, labor, income, taxes, earn, wages,* and many others.

In a math class in which students are studying a unit on geometry, students use such terms as *right angle, congruent, horizontal, vertical, intersect, reflection, symmetric,* and others to learn and communicate about their learning. In science class, technical vocabulary can be one of the major stumbling blocks to learning. Few children bring to school with them the knowledge of such terms as *adaptation, life cycle, diversity, organism, species, environmental,* and *genetic.* In art, music, and physical education classes, teachers have the opportunity to help students add words to their word stores such as *endurance, procedure, flexibility, performance, production, canvas, contrast,* and *exhibit.*

As mentioned previously, students should add approximately 1,000 to 3,000 new words to their meaning vocabulary stores each school year. Many of the new words they must learn are part of the specialized language needed to make sense of and communicate concepts in math, science, social studies, physical education, and the arts. If all teachers are on board to emphasize and use language in all classrooms, students' vocabularies will grow, and their learning in all subject areas will increase.

Teachers Include Writing in Every Subject

Think about the writing you did when you were in school or the writing you required of your students when teaching in a subject area. Most adults remember writing reports and answers to essay questions on tests. These traditional kinds of writing are primarily assessments; however, there is another kind of writing that teachers can use to promote learning. These are called *quick-writing activities* or *quick-writes.* Many teachers use learning logs for this purpose. Each day, students make a short entry in their log. The following are some learning-log prompts. Notice the different kinds of thinking these prompts require, including some higher-level thinking.

Learning-log prompts from a science class:

- "This week we will be learning about the water cycle—where water comes from, where it goes. I am going to give you two minutes to write down what you think you know about the water cycle. At the end of the lesson, you will add to what you know. Your two minutes start now."

- "Look back at what you wrote in your learning log. What things did we learn today that you were right about? What ideas did you have that were not true? Cross things out and add things to show what you now know about the water cycle."

- "Today you will create a diagram to show how the water cycle works. Your diagram should have pictures and labels. You may want to use arrows to show how the cycle works."

Learning-log prompts from a social studies class:

- "We are about to start a unit on the continents. I know you already know some things about them. You have three minutes to write down what you know about the seven continents. You can write the names of any you know and list anything you think you know beneath them. Remember that as we learn about the continents, you can return to your entry to correct, change, and add information, so don't be afraid to put down something you are not quite sure of."

- "I can tell you are all eager to get to your learning logs. Begin by correcting any information that you have learned was not true. Then add new facts that we learned today."

- "Today you will use your imaginations. Pretend that you can live for a year on any of the six other continents we have studied besides North America, the one we live on. Pick the continent you would go to and list all the reasons for your choice. In ten minutes, we will circle up and see which continents you chose and the reasons for those choices."

There are other ways to engage students in writing so that they think more actively about what they are learning. Some teachers begin each class with an "admit slip"—a prompt that asks students to review what they previously learned or has them looking ahead to what they will be learning. Students spend the first five minutes of class writing on the prompt. Some examples of admit-slip prompts include the following:

- "Last Friday, we took a virtual field trip to China and learned about how the country is rapidly modernizing. Write down some things you remember from last Friday's class."

- "We are starting a new unit on fractions this week in math. Think of ways we use fractions in our daily lives. Write down all the ways you can think of that fractions are used."

- "Today we are going to learn about Andy Warhol and how his paintings in the 1960s changed the way we view painting. Here are three of his most famous paintings. Write down what you notice about these paintings, how you think they are different, and why you think some people were shocked by these paintings."

Another strategy is the "exit slip," which students complete as their ticket to leave class. Some examples include the following:

- "Write down the three most interesting things you learned today."

- "If you could talk with Amelia Earhart, what three questions would you ask her?"

- "We learned a lot about animals and how they adapt to their environments. Write down the animal you find most fascinating and three reasons why."

When students write, they have to think—they recall facts, analyze events, apply ideas to real life, evaluate and form opinions, and create things. Two major reviews of research (Bangert-Drowns, Hurley, & Wilkinson, 2004; Graham & Perin, 2007) found that students who wrote during science, social studies, and other subjects increased their learning in those subjects.

Teachers Include Research and Inquiry for Learning Content

A research- and inquiry-based approach to instruction asks students to use reading to discover and learn content. This method calls for students to access a variety of texts—books, magazines, and web sources, for example—to answer questions about content that students themselves or teachers have formulated. Students can then work together in teams to gather information or data to help them answer questions. This approach to content instruction requires students to do a lot of purposeful reading, and it's usually higher-level thinking because the questions they are investigating are seldom who, what, when, and where factual questions. Teams of students find, read, and evaluate sources together, which provides scaffolding for reading, and teachers can assist and support students as needed. In most inquiry learning, students create a product or make a presentation to share what they have learned with their classmates. Teachers who include research and inquiry in their instruction are teaching students how to use the language skills of listening, speaking, writing, and reading to learn content.

Teachers Provide Guidance and Instruction for Common Texts

As you think about how content-area teachers use language and literacy within the curriculum in your school, consider what teachers do when all students are reading a common text. Do you see round-robin, taking turns oral reading and answering of low-level factual questions? Or do you see questioning and discussion that focus students on big ideas and engage them in higher-level thinking?

Subject-area teachers do not need to know all the things about reading that reading teachers know. They don't need to know how to teach phonics or build fluency or set up good independent reading programs. Subject-area teachers need to know how to focus their students' attention on what they want them to learn from an informational text. They also need to understand that informational texts are structured differently than fiction, and students often need guidance in following the structure of those texts.

Research supports setting content purposes and providing instruction on text structures to help students increase both motivation and comprehension (Guthrie et al., 2006). Ramsay and Sperling (2010) cite several studies showing that giving students good prereading questions or establishing a specific task or purpose for reading can increase both student interest and comprehension. When teachers give students tasks to preview before reading (that they will complete after reading), student monitoring of their own learning improves (Thiede, Wiley, & Griffin, 2011).

Graphic organizers that capture the way the important ideas are structured in an assigned text (Goldman & Rakestraw, 2000) are perhaps the most helpful lesson frameworks for subject-area teachers to incorporate into their instruction. For example, guided by the teacher, students reading about China can preview the text and construct a web skeleton. As they read, they can add information to the spokes of the web. Students studying American history can construct timelines to record important dates and events, such as the Revolutionary War. Students can use Venn diagrams or data charts to compare and contrast information, such as the traditions and holidays of different cultural groups. Causal chains can help students determine causes and effects during science instruction, such as with climate change.

It is important, however, that graphic organizers do not become just one more worksheet for students to complete. Students should learn to determine which type of organizer is best to arrange information from a particular text and then create the organizer—not just fill in blanks on a worksheet. Allowing students to work together to create organizers is valuable because the interaction fosters the development of language skills through listening and speaking.

Resources for Content-Area Literacy Study Groups

When content-area teachers include more intentional listening, speaking, reading, and writing in their lessons, students are the beneficiaries. This focus will not take time and energy away from content learning; rather, incorporating language skills will increase students' learning of the content. As you observe teachers in the classroom and evaluate lesson plans and schedules, it is helpful to look for the indicators that students are learning how to use the language of each subject area to comprehend and communicate.

If improving content-area literacy in your school is one of your priorities, see the reproducible resources list on pages 49–50. These resources provide detailed descriptions and lesson templates that will help teachers overcome the roadblocks and implement the best practices described in this chapter. Articles from *The Reading Teacher* are included because they are quick reads that can launch your discussions and because they are accessible online with a subscription.

The State of Content-Area Literacy Instruction in Your School

This chapter has answered three important questions about content-area literacy: What misconceptions act as roadblocks in the way of implementing better content-area literacy instruction? What does good content-area literacy instruction look like? What specific resources could you use to help teachers improve their content-area literacy instruction?

Compared with other areas of reading, content-area literacy instruction may be a relative weakness or strength in your school. To help you decide whether you need to intervene with some or all of your teachers with a study group or other professional development, we have compiled an informal checklist (page 51) for considering the state of content-area literacy instruction in your school. If you decide an intervention is needed in content-area literacy instruction, you may find the same checklist useful to help you determine the effectiveness of the intervention.

Content-Area Literacy Resources

This resource contains 7,932 words drawn from all areas of the curriculum, a six-step procedure for teaching vocabulary, and games and other activities for review:

- Marzano, R. J., & Pickering, D. J. (2005). *Building academic vocabulary: Teacher's manual.* Alexandria, VA: Association for Supervision and Curriculum Development.

This book contains general vocabulary strategies and a separate chapter devoted to building academic vocabulary in math, science, social studies, and the arts:

- Cunningham, P. M. (2009). *What really matters in vocabulary: Research-based practices across the curriculum.* Boston: Pearson.

The following resources contain ways to guide students through informational text and ideas for incorporating writing into subject-area lessons:

- Daniels, H., & Harvey, S. (2009). *Comprehension & collaboration: Inquiry circles in action.* Portsmouth, NH: Heinemann.
- Harvey, S., & Goudvis, A. (2007). *Strategies that work: Teaching comprehension for understanding and engagement* (2nd ed.). Portland, ME: Stenhouse.
- Moss, B., & Loh, V. (2010). *35 strategies for guiding readers through informational text.* New York: Guilford Press.
- Murphey, D. (2010). *You can't just say it louder! Differentiated strategies for comprehending nonfiction.* Huntington Beach, CA: Shell Education.

These resources contain content-specific lesson templates and examples for teaching vocabulary in grades 1–8:

- Dugan, C. (2010). *Strategies for building academic vocabulary in mathematics.* Huntington Beach, CA: Shell Education.
- Dugan, C. (2010). *Strategies for building academic vocabulary in science.* Huntington Beach, CA: Shell Education.
- Dugan, C. (2010). *Strategies for building academic vocabulary in social studies.* Huntington Beach, CA: Shell Education.

These resources contain content-specific lesson templates and examples for teaching comprehension in grades 1–8:

- Brummer, T., & Macceca, S. (2008). *Reading strategies for mathematics.* Huntington Beach, CA: Shell Education.
- Daniels, H., & Steineke, N. (2010). *Texts and lessons for content-area reading.* Portsmouth, NH: Heinemann.
- Macceca, S. (2007). *Reading strategies for science.* Huntington Beach, CA: Shell Education.
- Macceca, S. (2007). *Reading strategies for social studies.* Huntington Beach, CA: Shell Education.

The following are practical articles on literacy strategies across the curriculum:

- Akhondi, M., Malayeri, F. A., & Samad, A. A. (2011). How to teach expository text structure to facilitate reading comprehension. *The Reading Teacher, 64*(5), 368–372.
- Blachowicz, C., & Obrochtav, C. (2005). Vocabulary visits: Virtual field trips for content vocabulary development. *The Reading Teacher, 59*(3), 262–268.
- Bluestein, N. A. (2010). Unlocking text features for determining importance in expository text: A strategy for struggling readers. *The Reading Teacher, 63*(7), 597–600.
- Cummins, S., & Stallmeyer-Gerard, C. (2011). Teaching for synthesis of informational texts with read-alouds. *The Reading Teacher, 64*(6), 394–405.
- Dymock, S., & Nicholson, T. (2010). "High 5!" Strategies to enhance comprehension of expository text. *The Reading Teacher, 64*(3), 166–178.

- Fisher, D., Frey, N., & Lapp, D. (2008). Shared readings: Modeling comprehension, vocabulary, text structures, and text features for older readers. *The Reading Teacher, 61*(7), 548–556.

- Ikpeze, C. H., & Boyd, F. B. (2007). Web-based inquiry learning: Facilitating thoughtful literacy with Webquests. *The Reading Teacher, 60*(7), 644–654.

- Kelley, J. G., Lesaux, N. K., Kieffer, M. J., & Faller, S. E. (2010). Effective academic vocabulary instruction in the urban middle school. *The Reading Teacher, 64*(1), 5–14.

- Kelley, M. J., & Clausen-Grace, N. (2010). Guiding students through expository text with text feature walks. *The Reading Teacher, 64*(3), 191–195.

- Knipper, K. J., & Duggan, T. J. (2006). Writing to learn across the curriculum: Tools for comprehension in content area classes. *The Reading Teacher, 59*(5), 462–470.

- Moss, B. (2005). Making a case and a place for effective content area literacy instruction in the elementary grades. *The Reading Teacher, 59*(1), 46–55.

- Neufeld, P. (2005). Comprehension instruction in content area classes. *The Reading Teacher, 59*(4), 302–321.

- Ogle, D., & Correa-Kovtun, A. (2010). Supporting English-language learners and struggling readers in content literacy with the "partner reading and content, too" routine. *The Reading Teacher, 63*(7), 532–542.

- Pierce, M. E., & Fontaine, M. L. (2009). Designing vocabulary instruction in mathematics. *The Reading Teacher, 63*(3), 239–243.

- Putman, M. S., & Kingsley, T. (2009). The atoms family: Using podcasts to enhance the development of science vocabulary. *The Reading Teacher, 63*(2), 100–108.

- Raphael, T. E., & Au, K. H. (2005). QAR: Enhancing comprehension and test taking across grades and content areas. *The Reading Teacher, 59*(3), 206–221.

- Stahl, K. A. D., & Bravo, M. A. (2010). Contemporary classroom vocabulary assessment for content areas. *The Reading Teacher, 63*(7), 566–578.

- Spencer, B. H., & Guillaume, A. M. (2006). Integrating curriculum through the learning cycle: Content-based reading and vocabulary instruction. *The Reading Teacher, 60*(3), 206–219.

- Wilcox, B., & Monro, E. (2011). Integrating writing and mathematics. *The Reading Teacher, 64*(7), 521–529.

Content-Area Literacy Instruction: What to Look For

As you observe in classrooms and examine lesson plans and class schedules, ask the following questions about what you see, hear, and read:

1. Do your teachers teach the academic or technical vocabulary in every subject they teach?

   ☐ Frequently ☐ Occasionally ☐ Rarely ☐ Never

   Comments:

2. Do your teachers include writing, especially quick-writes, to help students learn content?

   ☐ Frequently ☐ Occasionally ☐ Rarely ☐ Never

   Comments:

3. Do your teachers include student research and inquiry to help students learn content?

   ☐ Frequently ☐ Occasionally ☐ Rarely ☐ Never

   Comments:

4. When teachers have students read a common text, do they provide comprehension instruction on that text?

   ☐ Frequently ☐ Occasionally ☐ Rarely ☐ Never

   Comments:

FIVE

PHONICS

In 1955, Rudolf Flesch published *Why Johnny Can't Read*, which quickly became a best seller. In this book, Flesch, a journalist, described how his friend's twelve-year-old son couldn't read until he was taught phonics. From this one example, Flesch concluded that the lack of phonics instruction in U.S. public schools was a national problem and the reason for all school failure. The public and some educators latched on to this seemingly simple solution to a complex problem, and it has been a point of controversy ever since.

Phonics is making connections between letters and sounds. There is no doubt that children need instruction in phonics and that some children who struggle with reading need more phonics instruction than others, but it is also clear that phonics by itself is not the answer for reaching the goal of all children reading at grade level. As documented earlier, Reading First was primarily a phonics initiative that was widely and faithfully implemented and failed to produce real gains in reading achievement. After testing Flesch's hypothesis in the years since Reading First was implemented, we can now definitely state that phonics, by itself, will not cure our national reading malaise.

The Roadblocks to Phonics Instruction

Good phonics instruction is an important component of a comprehensive reading program. Unfortunately, phonics has often been the tail wagging the dog. Here are some of the phonics roadblocks commonly impeding good, balanced literacy programs.

Too Much Instructional Time Spent on Phonics

Reading First mandated that school systems receiving federal money implement a research-based curriculum. In reality, that meant that most school systems had to choose a commercial reading program with highly decodable text for the primary grades. The scripted instruction in these programs focused on teaching children phonics skills, with little concern for meaning vocabulary or comprehension. If a teacher followed the scripting, most of the instructional time was spent teaching phonics and phonemic awareness. In chapter 1, we described the research Juel and her colleagues (2003) carried out with 200 children from low-socioeconomic backgrounds. As preschoolers, almost all of these students demonstrated deficits in both phonics and meaning vocabulary. Most of the instruction they received was phonics instruction, and it was effective; by the middle of first grade, most of the children no longer had a phonics deficit. However, except for the children whose teacher emphasized both phonics and meaning vocabulary, all the children still had a vocabulary deficit.

In a classroom, time is like money: spend most of it on one thing and there is little left for other things. Beginning readers need phonics instruction, but if that is the only instruction they receive, they will learn to decode words, but they will not build the meaning vocabularies and comprehension strategies necessary for understanding what the words they have decoded mean.

Overemphasizing Phonemic Awareness in Kindergarten

From their early encounters with reading and writing, children come to understand that spoken words are made up of sounds. These sounds (phonemes) are not separate and distinct. In fact, they are quite abstract. Phonemic awareness has many levels and includes the concept of rhyme and the ability to blend and segment words and to manipulate phonemes to form different words. Children who have been read to and who have been exposed to songs, nursery rhymes, and books with rhymes and alliteration usually enter school with adequately developing phonemic awareness skills.

Phonemic awareness is one of the best predictors of success in learning to read (Ehri & Nunes, 2002; National Reading Panel, 2000). This leads some to conclude that phonemic awareness is all teachers need to focus on in preschool and kindergarten. Phonemic awareness training programs mandate that every child have thirty to forty minutes of phonemic instruction every day; this leaves less time for other crucial prereading instruction, such as developing print tracking skills, learning some letter names and sounds, developing cognitive clarity about what reading and writing are for, and building a meaning vocabulary. Yopp and Yopp (2000) argue for phonemic awareness instruction as only *one* part of a beginning literacy program:

> Our concern is that in some classrooms phonemic awareness instruction will replace other crucial areas of instruction. Phonemic awareness supports reading development only if it is part of a broader program that includes—among other things—development of students' vocabulary, syntax, comprehension, strategic reading abilities, decoding strategies, and writing across all content areas. (p. 142)

The research on teaching phonemic awareness suggests that even the children who need such instruction should receive no more than eighteen hours total (about thirty minutes per week). After that amount of instruction, little additional learning occurs (National Reading Panel, 2000). Restricting phonemic awareness instruction to that research-based amount would leave ample time for a broader program.

The Belief That Phonics Instruction Is Not Needed After Second Grade

Look at the following words and think about what phonics knowledge is needed to decode them: *insubstantial, credibility, internationalize*. The first thing to notice is that you can't pronounce each letter and blend those sounds together to figure them out. Second, you realize that the vowel rules that apply to monosyllabic words don't work with polysyllabic words. Most polysyllabic words are root words with prefixes and suffixes added to the beginnings and ends. *Insubstantial* is the word *substance* with the suffix *ial*, which changes it from a noun to an adjective. The prefix *in* denotes its opposite meaning. Many English words, including *partial, sequential*, and *presidential*, end in *ial*. These words are all related to the root words *part, sequence*, and *president*, and the *ial* always has the same pronunciation and changes the word from a noun to an adjective. The prefix *in* at the beginning of many words—*insensitive, inconclusive, insecure*—changes the meaning of the base word to its opposite meaning. *Credibility* is the quality of being credible, and the suffix has the same pronunciation and meaning relation as it does in other words—*able, ability; noble, nobility; possible, possibility. Internationalize* shares the prefix *inter*, meaning "between," with other words, including *intersection* and *interplanetary*. The suffixes *al* and *ize* are pronounced and have the same meanings as they do in *natural, modernize*, and *personalize*.

In chapter 3, we described how readers use the context of what they are reading along with morphology to figure out the meaning of unfamiliar words they encounter in reading. Morphology does give us clues to the meanings of words, but it also is the link we use to decode words. When we teach students to look for morphological links in unfamiliar words, we are teaching them the phonics skills they need to decode polysyllabic words. Very few polysyllabic words occur in readings at the second-grade level. If all phonics instruction must be completed by the end of second grade, we will not be teaching students how to decode longer words, which make up the bulk of the new words they encounter from third grade on.

The Belief That All Children Who Struggle Lack Phonics Skills

It is probable that Flesch's friend's twelve-year-old son needed phonics instruction; when he received it, he became a good reader. For many older struggling readers, however, a lack of phonics skills is not the problem.

In 1998, test results in Washington State indicated that 43 percent of fourth-grade students had not met proficiency on the state reading assessment. The Washington State Legislature allocated $9,000,000 to K–2 classrooms to be used for instructional materials and professional development focused on research-based beginning reading strategies. As a result, districts were encouraged to adopt instructional materials and approaches that emphasized phonics.

Buly and Valencia (2002) did reading profiles on a sample of 108 of the fourth graders who scored below proficiency on the state assessment. They found that less than half of these struggling readers had a weakness in word identification. The researchers concluded that:

> Mandating phonics instruction . . . for all students who fall below proficiency would miss large numbers of students (more than 50% in our sample) whose word identification skills are fairly strong yet who struggle with comprehension, fluency or language. (p. 233)

A more recent study by Lesaux and Kieffer (2010) confirms these results. They gave a standardized reading comprehension test to 581 urban sixth graders and found that 45 percent scored at or below the thirty-fifth percentile. These 262 struggling readers were then given a battery of tests to determine their relative strengths and weaknesses on the major components of reading. Decoding was above average for 79 percent of the struggling readers and a relative strength for the majority of the rest. Fluency was at least average or a relative strength for the majority of the students. What the struggling readers had most in common was low meaning vocabulary knowledge. The researchers concluded that the near exclusive focus under Reading First on phonics and fluency was inadequate to prevent readers from struggling or to teach them what they would need to know to be able to comprehend satisfactorily when they reached middle school.

Best Practices for Phonics Instruction

Once you know what to look for—both the roadblocks and best practices—you can determine how well teachers are teaching phonics in your school. Look for these best practices that indicate your teachers are teaching phonics well as one part of a comprehensive reading curriculum.

Phonemic Awareness Is *One* Part of Kindergarten Instruction

Many children enter kindergarten with well-developed phonemic awareness skills. These children come from literate homes in which their parents and other adults read to them and engage them with songs, nursery rhymes, and conversation. Through these interactions with language, children develop a host of abilities, including phonemic awareness. They can track print and read some words—typically those that have personal importance. They can name many of the letters and often write them, usually in capital letters. They have more words in their meaning vocabulary stores, and their ability to comprehend what someone reads to them is excellent. They know what reading is for and are eager to learn to read.

What should a kindergarten classroom provide for children who come to school who haven't had these literacy encounters and who lack phonemic awareness? Common sense tells us that if kindergarten is going to prepare all children to be successful readers, it should re-create the language activities that children from literate homes experience.

Kindergarten teachers should read many books, not just during the scheduled read-aloud time, but throughout the day as well, and use the books read aloud to build meaning vocabulary and comprehension skills. Teachers should also engage students in shared reading while making sure they pay attention to the printed words and learn how to track them. Children can learn and repeat songs, nursery rhymes, and chants that are recorded on charts to build familiarity. Students who are still unaware of phonemes after a steady diet of such experiences can be grouped together and given more systematic phonemic awareness instruction for five to ten minutes per day.

When examining the instruction and lesson plans of kindergarten teachers, look at how time is being used throughout the day and be sure there is ample opportunity for children to grow in all areas of literacy development, including phonemic awareness.

Teachers Also Emphasize Meaning Vocabulary and Comprehension in Primary Grades

In most schools, first and second graders are tested on their ability to decode nonsense words and on the number of words they can pronounce correctly in one minute. Thus, it's no surprise that phonics instruction occupies the majority of the instructional time in many first- and second-grade classrooms. In addition, the programs currently used to teach reading in most schools have a narrow focus on phonics in grades one and two.

In chapter 2, we indicated that one of the roadblocks to comprehension instruction is that comprehension often has to "wait its turn" after phonics instruction. We suggested that principals observe reading instruction in the primary grades to be sure students are reading for simple purposes, such as picking their favorite part of a text or deciding what is the most interesting thing they learned. Making sure students—and teachers—never lose sight of comprehension as the purpose for reading decreases the possibility of an overemphasis on phonics that can lead to students who sound fluent but do not think about what they are reading.

Because of the pressure to increase reading scores in primary grades, it's not uncommon for schools to reduce the amount of instructional time spent on science and social studies. It is understandable that primary grade teachers want to put most of their time and energy into teaching the knowledge on which their students are assessed; however, this approach fails to look at the big picture. It may result in increased test scores in primary grades, but it almost surely results in large numbers of children scoring below grade level in reading in upper grades when comprehension and meaning vocabulary—not word identification—are what students must demonstrate. Many unfamiliar words and concepts for which students must build meaning reside in the subject areas of science and social studies. Students must receive comprehensive instruction, including on informational texts about science and social studies, from the very beginning—especially when a school has many students at risk for reading failure. Comprehension cannot be left to wait its turn.

Primary Grade Students Read a Variety of Texts

Along with the emphasis on phonics instruction, Reading First promoted programs that contained highly decodable text: "artificial" text written so students can apply the phonics skills they are learning, with the number of nondecodable words limited to those that are essential to creating sentences. The following are two examples:

Pal has Ham.

Lil has a big ham. Bill has a big pot. Bill can fill the pot. See the big pot hiss! Bill has ham. Lil has ham. Pal has a big ham. (Curran, 2006)

Will Ron Fix his Rig?

Ron has a rig he can not fix. Dan has his kit to fix it. Dan can not fix it. Al has a kit to fix it. Al will go down to fix it. Will Al fix it up? Al can fix the rig. (Benjamin, 2006)

While it is important for students to apply the phonics they learn to their reading, a steady diet of decodable texts has unintended consequences: If children focus too much attention on decoding words, they may not learn to simultaneously attend to meaning. The words in highly decodable text often do not really mean anything—at least not to young children. The words are simply there for practice in decoding. Most six-year-olds would not know what *kit* or *rig* mean. When there is little meaning, children get in the habit of just saying words without thinking or caring about what they mean. This habit interferes with children's acquisition of new word meanings.

Principals should evaluate the materials first- and second-grade teachers use to teach reading. If most texts children are reading consist of highly decodable text, then it is critical that teachers begin to include other materials. Luckily, in most schools, leveled readers from a previous era are gathering dust in closets and storerooms, and classrooms are filled with appealing informational texts such as *TIME For Kids*, *Scholastic News*, and *Weekly Reader*. Many Internet sites, including Enchanted Learning (www.enchantedlearning.com), Reading A-Z (www.readinga-z.com), and Children's Storybooks Online (www.magickeys.com) have easy-to-read selections teachers can download and copy. Including these resources in instruction provides students with a more balanced reading diet and decreases the number of children who develop the habit of reading without thinking. Another advantage of including reproducible books is that, after reading them in class, students can take them home and add them to their personal reading libraries.

Primary Teachers Include Both Decoding and Encoding Activities

While *decoding* is using phonics to pronounce unfamiliar words, *encoding* is using phonics to spell unfamiliar words. The research is clear: children learn how to decode better in reading when their phonics instruction includes encoding as well as decoding instruction and practice (Weiser & Mathes, 2011). In their meta-analysis of studies, Weiser and Mathes found that children who manipulated letters to construct words or wrote words during phonics instruction learned to decode much better than children who had systematic decoding instruction alone. Another unfortunate consequence of Reading First was a decrease in emphasis on writing with phonics spelling (also called *invented spelling*). Research has found that invented spelling causes students to learn to read better (Ouellette & Sénéchal, 2008). Kindergarten, first-grade, and second-grade teachers should regularly help students apply phonics during encoding activities including word-making, spelling, and writing, as well as during more traditional decoding activities.

Upper-Grade Teachers Include Morphology Instruction

Teachers in the upper grades are probably not accustomed to teaching phonics; however, the phonics that students need to decode polysyllabic words such as *insubstantial, credibility,* and *internationalize* cannot be taught in primary grades where very few of these words occur. If upper-grade teachers are teaching students to use morphology and context to figure out the meaning of unfamiliar words, then they are also teaching them the tools they need to decode polysyllabic words. Many students in upper grades struggle with decoding and accessing meaning for the polysyllabic words that make up the majority of the unfamiliar words they encounter. Often, instead of trying to pronounce the words and figure out the meanings, they simply skip over them. Teaching students how to use roots, prefixes, and suffixes to decode and figure out meanings for polysyllabic words will remove a major stumbling block to comprehension in upper grades.

Resources for Phonics Study Groups

Children at all grade levels need instruction in phonics, but what they need varies greatly across grade levels. Kindergarteners need to develop phonemic awareness, the realization that spoken words are made up of sounds. First- and second-grade students should learn how to decode and spell short words. Older students need to learn to recognize familiar word parts— prefixes, suffixes, and roots—which are the keys to decoding, spelling, and understanding the meaning of polysyllabic words. Principals must ensure that phonemic awareness and phonics are not taking too much of the instructional time in kindergarten and the primary grades and that morphology is getting its share of instructional time in intermediate grades.

If improving phonics instruction in your school is one of your priorities, see the reproducible resources list on page 60. These resources provide detailed descriptions and lesson templates that will help your teachers overcome the roadblocks and implement the best practices described in this chapter. Articles from *The Reading Teacher* are included because they are quick reads that can launch your discussions and because they are accessible online with a subscription.

The State of Phonics Instruction in Your School

This chapter has answered three important questions about phonics: What misconceptions act as roadblocks in the way of implementing better phonics instruction? What does good phonics instruction look like? What specific resources could you use to help your teachers improve their phonics instruction?

Compared with other areas of reading, phonics instruction may be a relative weakness or strength in your school. To help you decide whether you need to intervene with some or all of your teachers with a study group or other professional development, we have compiled an informal checklist (page 61) for considering the state of phonics instruction in your school. If you decide an intervention is needed in phonics instruction, you may find the same checklist useful to help you determine the effectiveness of the intervention.

Phonics Resources

The following resources can be used to improve phonics instruction, particularly in the areas of encoding activities and using morphological clues to meaning and decoding:

- Bear, D., Invernizzi, M., Templeton, S., & Johnston, F. (2012). *Words their way: Word study for phonics, vocabulary, and spelling instruction* (5th ed.). Boston: Pearson.

- Cunningham, P. M. (2012). *What really matters in spelling: Research-based strategies and activities.* Boston: Pearson.

- Cunningham, P.M. (2013). *Phonics they use: Words for reading and writing* (6th ed.). Boston: Allyn & Bacon.

- Cunningham, P. M., & Hall, D. P. (2009). *Making words fifth grade: 50 hands-on lessons for teaching prefixes, suffixes and roots.* Boston: Allyn & Bacon.

- Cunningham, P. M., & Hall, D. P. (2009). *Making words fourth grade: 50 hands-on lessons for teaching prefixes, suffixes and roots.* Boston: Allyn & Bacon.

- Ganske, K. (2006). *Word sorts and more: Sound, pattern, and meaning explorations K–3.* New York: Guilford Press.

The following are practical articles on morphology published in *The Reading Teacher*:

- Gill, S. (2007). Learning about word parts with Kidspiration. *The Reading Teacher, 61*(1), 79–84.

- Kieffer, M. J., & Lesaux, N. K. (2007). Breaking down words to build meaning: Morphology, vocabulary, and reading comprehension in the urban classroom. *The Reading Teacher, 61*(2), 134–144.

- Mountain, L. (2005). ROOTing out meaning: More morphemic analysis for primary pupils. *The Reading Teacher, 58*(8), 742–749.

Phonics Instruction: What to Look For

As you observe in classrooms and examine lesson plans and class schedules, ask the following questions about what you see, hear, and read:

1. Do kindergarten teachers facilitate the development of phonemic awareness as well as the other early reading concepts?

    ☐ Frequently   ☐ Occasionally   ☐ Rarely   ☐ Never

    Comments:

2. Do primary-grade teachers emphasize meaning vocabulary and comprehension as well as phonics?

    ☐ Frequently   ☐ Occasionally   ☐ Rarely   ☐ Never

    Comments:

3. Do primary-grade teachers include a variety of kinds of text in their reading instruction?

    ☐ Frequently   ☐ Occasionally   ☐ Rarely   ☐ Never

    Comments:

4. Do primary-grade teachers include both decoding and encoding activities as part of their phonics instruction?

    ☐ Frequently   ☐ Occasionally   ☐ Rarely   ☐ Never

    Comments:

5. Do upper-grade teachers include instruction in morphology?

    ☐ Frequently   ☐ Occasionally   ☐ Rarely   ☐ Never

    Comments:

SIX

FLUENCY

Sometimes in order to understand what something is, you have to understand what it is not. To experience what it feels like to read without fluency, read the following paragraph aloud *without* first reading it to yourself. When you have finished reading it, cover it and then summarize what you read aloud.

FLUENCYISTHEABILITYTOREADMOSTWORDSINCONTEXTQUICKLYANDACCURATELY
ANDWITHAPPROPRIATEEXPRESSIONFLUENCYISCRITICALTOREADINGCOMPREHEN
SIONBECAUSEOFTHEATTENTIONFACTOROURBRAINSCANATTENDTOALIMITEDNUM
BEROFTHINGSATATIMEIFMOSTOFOURATTENTIONISFOCUSEDONDECODINGTH
EWORDSTHEREISLITTLEATTENTIONLEFTFORTHECOMPREHENSIONPARTOFREADING
PUTTINGTHEWORDSTOGETHERANDTHINKINGABOUTWHATTHEYMEAN

If you paused to figure out several of the words, and if your phrasing and expression were not very smooth, you experienced what it feels like to be able to read something accurately, but not fluently. If your summary lacked important information, you experienced the detrimental effects of a lack of fluency on comprehension. If you are beginning to develop a headache, you have experienced what a painful task reading can be to readers who lack fluency.

Fluency is the ability to orally read most words in context quickly and accurately and with appropriate expression. Fluency is critical to reading comprehension because of the attention factor. Our brains can only attend to a limited number of things at a time. If most of our attention is focused on decoding the words there is little attention left for the comprehension part of reading—putting the words together and thinking about what they mean.

The paragraph you just read is exactly the same as the one written on this page in caps with no punctuation and no spaces between words. If, this time, you read it quickly and effortlessly and with good comprehension, you read it fluently.

In order to become avid and enthusiastic readers who get pleasure and information from reading, children must develop fluency. Children who have to labor over most of what they read will only read when forced to and will never understand how anyone can actually enjoy reading.

The Roadblocks to Fluency

In chapter 1, we described how assessment can promote or hinder good instruction. Words-correct-per-minute measures that purport to measure fluency but actually just measure speed are a prime example of how assessment that is not valid hinders good instruction. This faux fluency assessment, along with the lack of easy reading for struggling readers, are the two major roadblocks to good fluency instruction.

Fluency Assessments Don't Always Measure Fluency

Fluency assessment has become a regular part of literacy instruction since the National Reading Panel (NRP) recommended that fluency be assessed and response to intervention (RTI) mandated regular assessment of reading skills, including fluency. In many classrooms, however, fluency is measured by the number of words correct per minute (WCPM) a child reads. In chapter 1, we pointed out that many people, including Jay Samuels (2007), a top expert on automaticity and fluency in reading and a member of the NRP, do not consider these WCPM measures to be valid measures of fluency:

> One criticism I have of the DIBELS tests is that, despite their labels, they are not valid tests of the construct of fluency as it is widely understood and defined. They only assess accuracy and speed. By attaching the term fluency to their tests, they create the false assumption that that is what the tests measure. (p. 564)

It does not matter if an assessment is quick and easy to administer if it doesn't measure what it is intended to measure and doesn't help us make wise instructional decisions. If a child does not read enough words correctly in one minute, is that because that child misread a lot of words and thus may need more phonics instruction? Did the reader stop to successfully figure out a word or go back to self-correct an earlier error, and did these good reading strategies result in fewer words read correctly in a minute? Savvy students quickly figure out that they will get a better score on the DIBELS and similar tests if they just skip any word they don't immediately recognize. There is no penalty for skipping words, and since there is no comprehension check, it doesn't matter at all whether or not students understand what they are reading. Rate is being measured, but accuracy may not be.

In addition to speed and accuracy, fluency always includes expression. We say a person is a fluent reader if his or her oral reading "sounds like speech." Reading with expression is a critical part of fluency because it is evidence of comprehension, and good phrasing itself promotes comprehension. It is important to measure students' fluency, but educators must add a measure of expression and comprehension to WCPM assessments if we truly want to know how fluently students are reading.

Struggling Readers Rarely Read Anything Easy

Most of the reading we do is not at our reading level. In fact, most of what we read is much too easy for us. If your reading in the past month has included the latest bestselling novel, a travel guide in preparation for an upcoming trip, a journal article on effective leadership strategies, and your favorite section of the local newspaper, all this reading was most likely at your independent level. Because these are all things you chose to read and were interested in, you had large amounts of background knowledge for these topics, and you instantly recognized at least 99 percent of the words.

The best readers—those whose instructional reading levels are above the grade level they are placed in—also spend most of their time reading text that is very easy for them. The science and social studies textbooks in their desks are written at the average reading level for their grade, but they are usually easy for the best readers, who read above grade level. The books and magazine articles they choose to read for independent reading at home and in school are also probably very easy for them. In fact, the best readers became fluent readers by reading and rereading lots of easy books.

Now think about the materials struggling readers are reading. They probably have the same grade-level science and social studies books in their desks as the best readers, and these books are much too hard for them to read. Hopefully, the books used for reading lessons are at their level—but that doesn't mean they are easy. The instructional reading level of most children is determined to be the level at which they can read 90 to 95 percent of the words and can comprehend 75 percent of the ideas. Even in material that is determined to be at their instructional reading level, children will encounter a word they don't recognize every two or three sentences. When they encounter these unfamiliar words, they have to stop and use whatever decoding strategies they know to figure out the words. This stopping to decode interrupts their fluency and interferes with comprehension.

Our best readers are fluent readers who spend a huge proportion of their reading time reading materials that are easy for them. Our struggling readers spend a huge proportion of their reading time struggling through text that is much too hard and a little bit of time working to read material that is at their instructional level. When reading both the too-hard text and the on-their-level text, they have to expend energy on decoding, and their reading usually lacks fluency. All students need regular easy reading—reading in which they don't have to figure out more than an occasional word and can concentrate all their attention on the ideas, forgetting that they are even reading.

Best Practices for Fluency Instruction

To determine how well your school is producing fluent readers, you need to look at how fluency is being assessed and what teachers are doing to ensure that all students are doing some reading that is easy for them. Once you know what to look for—both the roadblocks and best practices—you can determine how well teachers are promoting fluency in your school. The following best practices for fluency contribute to an effective reading program.

Fluency Measures That Actually Assess Fluency

The obvious advantage of WCPM measures is that they are quick and simple to administer: you listen to a student read, check the words read correctly, and count the checks at the end of a minute. While we are generally in favor of making things quick and easy for teachers, in this case, we suggest three adjustments to the WCPM measures to get a truly accurate assessment of how fluently students are reading:

1. To determine what kind of strategies a reader is using and what kind of errors he or she is making, the teacher should make a record of the errors—rather than just checking words read correctly. The teacher can then circle any words the child skips, and use a caret above the line to indicate any insertion, substitution, or mispronunciation errors. The teacher can also put an *H* above words that the child hesitates on and then correctly decodes so that the teacher will know which words the student is successfully decoding. Sometimes, students make an error and then go back and correct that error. This is a very good sign because it means they are monitoring their reading and realizing when something they read does not make sense. Teachers can note these self-corrections by writing a *C* above the word.

2. As each student reads and the teacher is recording the reading, the teacher should also listen for phrasing and expression. He or she can use a simple four-point scale to make a judgment about the expression aspect of fluency. Table 5.1 shows such a scale.

Table 5.1: Four-Point Oral Reading Expression Scale

Level 4	Reads in phrases with expression that sounds like speech
Level 3	Reads mostly in phrases and with some expression
Level 2	Reads mostly word by word with some phrases but little expression
Level 1	Reads like reading words in a list, word by word, and with little or no expression

3. Before students read the passage, the teacher should tell them to think about what they read because they will be asked to retell the major facts or events of what they read. When a student finishes reading, the teacher takes the passage away and asks the student to tell everything he or she remembers from the reading. The teacher listens while the student retells the information and then asks questions if unsure of how much the student comprehended. The student's comprehension is then rated on a four-point scale as shown in table 5.2.

Table 5.2: Four-Point Comprehension Scale

Level 4	Recalls most of the important events or facts and no misinformation
Level 3	Recalls a lot of events or facts and little misinformation
Level 2	Recalls some events or facts and may include some misinformation
Level 1	Recalls little except the topic

By adding these three components to the standard WCPM measures, teachers will truly measure fluency. They will know what kind of errors their students make in their reading and if they are self-correcting some of those errors when what they read does not make sense. Teachers will also be able to measure students' phrasing and expression, a critical component of fluency. Finally, teachers will know which students are thinking about what they read and which ones are just saying the words as fast as they can.

Teachers Model Good Expressive Oral Reading

Students need to hear good expressive reading modeled by their teachers. This may seem obvious, but in many classrooms, students go through the whole day without hearing anyone read in a fluent way. The most obvious opportunity for teachers to model fluent reading is when they are reading aloud to their students. Sadly, in this era of accountability, particularly in upper grades, reading aloud to students is a luxury teachers don't think they can afford. (In chapter 7, we provide more details about and support for reading aloud to students regularly in every classroom.) To help with fluency, principals need to determine which teachers are including read-alouds in their day, and when they read aloud, whether they are purposely reading with expression and phrasing and providing good oral reading models.

In addition to read-alouds, there are two other lesson formats that allow teachers to model expressive oral reading: echo reading and choral reading, both usually done with plays or poetry. In *echo reading*, the teacher reads a line or sentence well with expression. Students then are called on to echo the teacher's reading. In *choral reading*, groups of children are assigned different parts. They practice these parts together and then read them in chorus, focusing on rhythm and expression.

Look at the lesson plans of teachers in your school. Do you see at least one time slot each day for teacher read-alouds? Across a week's worth of reading lessons, do you see any plans for including echo and choral reading lessons using plays and poetry? If we want all our students to read fluently with proper phrasing and expression, we must provide models of what fluent reading sounds like.

Teachers Ensure That All Students Do Some Easy Reading

Most teachers know that their best readers spend a lot of their time reading easy things and their struggling readers rarely read anything easy. They also know that struggling readers resist reading and that it is hard to find any materials in which children who read below grade level can identify 98 to 99 percent of the words.

The first thing to look for to determine if all students are doing some easy reading is time in the daily schedule for independent reading. Like teacher read-aloud time, time for independent reading is often viewed as a luxury. Independent reading time, however, is the one opportunity teachers have to let children choose what they read. When children can choose and there is a wide range of materials to choose from, most will choose something easy. Independent reading and promoting easy reading for everyone will be discussed in more detail in the next chapter.

We can also provide easy reading for all students by creating opportunities for students to read the same text several times. The first time or two that students read a text, they will probably make errors and encounter words they cannot pronounce. With feedback and assistance, however, they should be reading the text almost perfectly on the last reading, and thus experience what easy reading feels like. There are two lesson formats for repeated readings that have demonstrated reading gains.

In 1998, Rasinski and Padak published a study that drew everyone's attention to how widespread fluency problems are for disabled readers. They looked at a large number of remedial readers and evaluated their abilities in comprehension, decoding, and fluency. Almost all the children were well below grade level in all three areas, but fluency was by far their greatest weakness. In response to their findings, Rasinski and Padak developed a lesson for teaching fluency: a fluency development lesson, or FDL (Rasinski & Padak, 2001).

In an FDL, the teacher chooses a short passage—often a poem—that is appealing to the students and then reads the passage aloud several times, modeling fluent reading. Meaning for the poem or passage and for any difficult vocabulary words is built through discussion. Next, the poem is read chorally several times, with different children reading different parts. The children are then paired and take turns reading the passage to each other, helping and supporting each other. Each partner reads the passage aloud three times.

The class gathers together again and reads the piece chorally one more time. Children put one copy of the text in their folder and are given a second copy to take home, where they read the passage to whoever will listen.

The following day, the previous day's passage is read again chorally and then the whole cycle begins with a new passage. When compared to children who read the same passages but did not use the FDL procedure, children in the FDL group made significantly greater gains in reading comprehension.

Fluency-oriented reading instruction (FORI; Stahl et al., 1997) is another lesson format in which students read a text multiple times. In FORI, the text is a longer passage from a reading program. Like FDL, the lesson begins with the teacher reading the text aloud while students follow along in their books. Following the teacher read-aloud, the class discusses the selection and the teacher builds vocabulary, comprehension, and other strategies related to the text. On the second day, the teacher and students do an echo reading of the selection. After the echo reading, students do some kind of comprehension activity, usually writing a short response. That night, students take the selection home to read to a family member. On the third day, students and teachers do a choral reading of the text. On the fourth day, students read the selection with a partner, taking turns reading each page. On the final day of the week, students do some extension activities related to the text.

Research on FORI (Stahl & Heubach, 2005) demonstrates gains made by the FORI students when compared with students at another school using the same commercial program but following the instructions in the teachers' guide instead of using the FORI procedures. Students whose reading instruction followed the FORI format made nearly two years of progress in one year of instruction.

In both FDL and FORI, teachers provide models of expressive reading and students read the text multiple times. By the last reading, most children are reading it almost perfectly and experiencing what it feels like to be a fluent reader.

Resources for Fluency Study Groups

As you observe teachers in the classroom and evaluate lesson plans and schedules, look for the indicators that your teachers are providing students with fluency instruction that will build their ability to read quickly, accurately, and with appropriate phrasing and expression.

If improving fluency instruction in your school is one of your priorities, see the reproducible resources list on page 70. These resources provide detailed descriptions and lesson templates that will help your teachers overcome the roadblocks and implement the best practices described in this chapter. Articles from *The Reading Teacher* are included because they are quick reads that can launch your discussions and because they are accessible online with a subscription.

The State of Fluency Instruction in Your School

This chapter has answered three important questions about fluency: What misconceptions act as roadblocks in the way of implementing better fluency instruction? What does good fluency instruction look like? What specific resources could you use to help your teachers improve their fluency instruction?

Compared with other areas of reading, fluency instruction may be a relative weakness or strength in your school. To help you decide whether you need to intervene with some or all of your teachers with a study group or other professional development, we have compiled an informal checklist (page 71) for considering the state of fluency instruction in your school. If you decide an intervention is needed in fluency instruction, you may find the same checklist useful to help you determine the effectiveness of the intervention.

Fluency Resources

The following books contain excellent suggestions for building and assessing fluency:

- Johns, J. L., & Berglund, R. L. (2010). *Fluency: Differentiated interventions and progress-monitoring assessments* (4th ed.). Dubuque, IA: Kendall Hunt.

- Rasinski, T., V. (2010). *The fluent reader: Oral & silent reading strategies for building fluency, word recognition & comprehension* (2nd ed.). New York: Scholastic Professional Books.

- Rasinski, T., & Griffith, L. (2012). *Fluency through practice and performance.* Huntington Beach, CA: Shell Education.

The following are practical articles on fluency from *The Reading Teacher*:

- Deeney, T. A. (2010). One-minute fluency measures: Mixed messages in assessment and instruction. *The Reading Teacher, 63*(6), 440–450.

- Griffith, L. W., & Rasinski, T. V. (2004). A focus on fluency: How one teacher incorporated fluency with her reading curriculum. *The Reading Teacher, 58*(2), 126–137.

- Marcell, B. (2012). Putting fluency on a fitness plan. *The Reading Teacher, 65*(4), 242–249.

- Morrow, L. M., Kuhn, M., & Schwanenflugel, P. (2006). The family fluency program. *The Reading Teacher, 60*(4), 322–333.

- Ness, M. (2009). Laughing through rereadings: Using joke books to build fluency. *The Reading Teacher, 62*(8), 691–694.

- Peebles, J. L. (2007). Incorporating movement with fluency instruction: A motivation for struggling readers. *The Reading Teacher, 60*(6), 578–581.

- Rasinski, T., Rupley, W. H., William, N., & William, D. (2008). Two essential ingredients: Phonics and fluency getting to know each other. *The Reading Teacher, 62*(3), 257–260.

- Rasinski, T., Rupley, W. H., Yildirim, K., & Nageldinger, J. (2012). Building fluency through the phrased text lesson. *The Reading Teacher, 65*(4), 252–255.

- Wilfong, L. G. (2008). Building fluency, word-recognition ability, and confidence in struggling readers: The poetry academy. *The Reading Teacher, 62*(1), 4–13.

- Young, C., & Rasinski, T. (2009). Implementing readers theatre as an approach to classroom fluency instruction. *The Reading Teacher, 63*(1), 4–13.

Fluency Instruction: What to Look For

As you observe in classrooms and examine lesson plans and class schedules, ask the following questions about what you see, hear, and read:

1. Do the fluency measures teachers use assess accuracy, expression, and comprehension as well as rate?

   ☐ Frequently   ☐ Occasionally   ☐ Rarely   ☐ Never

   Comments:

2. Do teachers model good expressive oral reading?

   ☐ Frequently   ☐ Occasionally   ☐ Rarely   ☐ Never

   Comments:

3. Do teachers ensure that all students, including struggling readers, do some easy reading?

   ☐ Frequently   ☐ Occasionally   ☐ Rarely   ☐ Never

   Comments:

SEVEN

TEACHER READ-ALOUD AND INDEPENDENT READING

The more you read, the better you read. Nagy and Anderson (1984) concluded that good readers read ten times as many words as struggling readers during the school day. Since struggling readers almost never choose to read at home, and good readers usually spend some time reading at home, the difference between the amount good readers read and the amount struggling readers read is likely much greater than this ten-to-one ratio. Stanovich, in his famous article "Matthew Effects in Reading" (1986), referred to the tendency of poor readers in early grades to remain poor readers throughout their school years as the "Matthew Effect." He attributed the increasing gap between good readers and poor readers in part to the difference in the amount of time spent reading. Guthrie and Humenick (2004) analyzed twenty-two studies of reading achievement and found that access to interesting books and choice of what to read were strongly correlated with reading achievement scores. In fact, they found that access and choice had larger effects on achievement than systematic phonics programs.

Why do children choose to read? In 1975, Sterl Artley asked college students what they remembered their teachers doing that motivated them to read. The majority of students reported that teachers reading aloud to them was the primary motivation for their choice to read when they were children. A 1994 study (Palmer, Codling, & Gambrell, 1994) asked elementary students what motivated them to read particular books. The most frequent response was "My teacher read it to the class." Ivey and Broaddus (2001) surveyed 1,765 sixth graders to determine what motivates them to read. The responses of this large, diverse group of preteens indicated that their major motivation for reading came from having time for independent reading of books of their own choosing and teachers reading aloud to them.

As described in chapter 2, most new word meanings children add to their vocabulary stores are learned as they encounter new words in their reading and figure out the meanings for those words. Children who read more have more opportunities to encounter new words and add new word meanings. Knowing meanings for key words enables comprehension, and lacking meanings hinders comprehension. Cunningham and Stanovich (1998) found that struggling readers with limited reading and comprehension achieved increased vocabulary and comprehension skills when time spent reading was increased. Lots of reading also increases the fluency with which children read. Students who read more encounter the same words (*they, which, could, for, of*) more frequently, and repeated exposure to the same words has been shown to lead to improvements in fluency (Topping & Paul, 1999).

Like multivitamins, teacher read-aloud and independent reading have benefits that cannot be easily observed. If you stop taking your vitamins for a month—or even a year—you will not see the effects immediately. We take our vitamins because we have faith that along with nutritious food and exercise, they will help promote and maintain our good health in the long run. Teacher read-aloud and independent reading are the daily multivitamins that, along with good instruction in comprehension, vocabulary, phonics, and fluency, promote optimum reading skills for all students.

The Roadblocks to Teacher Read-Aloud and Independent Reading

Since teacher read-aloud and independent reading have multiple benefits and are simple and enjoyable to implement, educators may wonder why they are so rarely seen in today's schools. The following are roadblocks that many schools experience when attempting to implement these strategies.

Teachers Think They Don't Have Time

The most common response principals hear from teachers when questioning why these strategies are not included in their daily schedules is that they don't have time. Even if you cannot increase the amount of time your teachers have, you can help them consider some alternatives to how they are using time. Some suggestions of where to find time for teacher read-aloud and independent reading are included in the next section.

The Benefits Are Not Easily Measured

We already mentioned that assessment can promote or hinder good instruction, and that, as Einstein said, some things that count cannot be easily counted. The benefits of teacher read-aloud and independent reading are a prime example. One way to indirectly measure the effects of teacher read-aloud and independent reading is to survey students early in the year about their reading interests and habits. Following are some questions teachers might use to establish a baseline for each student:

- The best book I ever read was _____. I liked it because _____.
- The best book I read in the last four months was _____. I liked it because _____.

- My favorite author is _____.

- My favorite kind of book is _____.

- When I am at home I read . . . (Circle one)

    Almost never   Sometimes   Almost every day   Every day

- This is how I feel about reading right now: (Circle one)

    I love reading.   I like reading.   I don't like reading.   I hate reading.

Teachers who are skeptical about the benefits of teacher read-aloud and independent reading but are willing to give it a try should do this survey with their students early in the school year, again at midyear, and at the end of the year. Teachers who believe that children either like to read or don't will be amazed at the change in attitude of some of their students and will have proof of the benefits of teacher read-aloud and independent reading.

The Belief That There Is No Supporting Research

Independent reading was dealt a near-fatal blow when the NRP concluded that there was no "scientific evidence" to support it (National Reading Panel, 2000). Of course, the NRP only permitted itself to examine experimental research (Cunningham, 2001), so it failed to find the long-term benefits of independent reading supported by other kinds of quantitative studies (see Anderson, Wilson, & Fielding, 1988; Cunningham & Stanovich, 1998; Hedrick & Cunningham, 2002; Nagy, Anderson, & Herman, 1987; Share, 2008). Not surprisingly, between the time Reading First—the program based on the NRP's findings—was implemented nationwide in 2002 and the NAEP Reading was administered in 2005, fourth graders' intrinsic motivation to read significantly declined (Perie, Grigg, & Donahue, 2005). Of course correlation is not causation, and we don't know that the drop in intrinsic motivation was caused by the types of instructional practices mandated by Reading First, but students who were in fourth grade in 2005 were the first group of children nationwide whose instruction was shaped by Reading First mandates.

Best Practices for Teacher Read-Aloud and Independent Reading

We hope that you are now convinced that teacher read-aloud and independent reading are not fluff but rather essential components of a comprehensive reading program. The following are the elements of effective instruction that includes teacher read-aloud and independent reading to help guide you in your assessment of the state of teacher read-aloud in your school.

Teachers Provide Read-Aloud and Independent Reading Daily

In many classrooms, you can determine that children are not being read to and given time to read materials of their choosing simply by looking at the posted schedules. In other classrooms, there is time allotted for these activities but this time gets siphoned into other activities for which there is more immediate accountability. Popping into classrooms during the time scheduled for teacher read-aloud and independent reading will let you know if these activities are actually happening.

Teachers are not simply making excuses when they declare that they don't have time or when they let the time get absorbed by other activities. Time really is a problem in virtually all classrooms. Teacher read-aloud and independent reading do not require huge allotments of time. Ten to fifteen minutes each day for teacher read-aloud and fifteen to twenty minutes for independent reading are probably sufficient. Remember that if these activities accomplish the big goal of motivating more children to read, children will extend that time and choose to read when they have a few minutes after they have finished their work and at home.

There are many ways to find relatively small amounts of time, which can then add up. What do children do when they arrive in the morning? In many classrooms, children complete morning work, which often consists of math or language worksheets. Working quietly at a desk on worksheets is not a very engaging way to start the school day. Teachers must consider how much is being learned with this activity. Usually, morning work is the same for everyone. Advanced children zip through it, and once finished, they often choose to read—these children clearly already have developed the reading habit. What does morning work accomplish for children who struggle? If the work is grade level, children who struggle with math or language skills usually can't successfully complete it. When children are working independently, they need to be able to complete the activity with a high success rate if that activity is going to help them grow (Rosenshine, 1983). A high success rate on independent work is rarely seen for the lowest achievers in any classroom. Because morning work is usually intended to practice grade-level skills, completing it only benefits the average children. For advanced and struggling readers, the time spent on morning work adds little, if any, value to their day.

What if instead of traditional morning work, students choose a book or magazine and read? With lots of materials available on a variety of levels, children could choose things they could read easily and experience what it feels like when reading is effortless. When the time for reading is up, two children each day (on a rotating schedule) could tell something they liked in their book, share their favorite page, or tell something they learned from that morning's reading. This quick book share further motivates children in their choice of what to read the following day. Teachers who use the first fifteen to twenty minutes of the day for independent reading time instead of worksheets report a happier, more successful start to their day—and fewer worksheets to grade!

Another option is to look at how time is used at the end of the day. In some classrooms, students spend fifteen minutes packing up. This time is often when classroom disruptions occur. Everyone—the teacher included—is tired, and the lack of structure during this time often results in an otherwise good day ending badly. Consider this alternative: Students spend five minutes packing up twenty minutes before the official end of the day. Children hurry to beat the clock and be in their seats with a book when the timer sounds. They then spend the last fifteen minutes reading, and the day comes to a quiet, peaceful end. This schedule has another advantage if students are called to the buses at different times. When independent reading time begins fifteen minutes before the first bus is called, everyone has fifteen minutes to read, and students with later buses have a few extra minutes of reading time.

The most unique solution to the problem of no time for independent reading was devised by a third-grade teacher in Charleston, South Carolina. After a grade-level meeting in which the need for independent reading was discussed, teachers were asked to give their schedules a fresh look and see where they could find fifteen minutes. After declaring that there were no wasted minutes in her day, she thought some more about it and came up with a solution. Students had to line up twice a day to be taken to the restrooms. The restrooms were small, so three boys and three girls went in at a time. This waiting was clearly wasted time. So the teacher gave children five minutes to choose something they wanted to read, and they carried their books and magazines down the hall to the restrooms where they sat in quiet lines reading while waiting their turn. This routine was repeated each morning and afternoon—resulting in about ten minutes of reading time twice each day for an additional one hundred minutes of reading time each week. An unexpected benefit was the near elimination of discipline problems while waiting.

Time for teacher read-aloud can also be found in unexpected places. In many classrooms, students have a snack time in the morning. Teachers who read to their students during snack time each day report that students enjoy both the snack and the reading and begin to associate the pleasure they experience in eating with the books they also enjoy.

Another place to find time for read-aloud is within subject areas. There are many wonderful books—both fiction and informational—that connect to science, social studies, and even math units. Reading books and magazine articles related to the topic being studied is another way for teachers to teach concepts and build academic vocabulary.

Another possibility for finding the thirty minutes to allot to teacher read-aloud and independent reading is to cut five minutes of instruction from each subject. If there are sixty minutes scheduled for math, change that to fifty-five. Writing could be shaved to forty minutes from forty-five. Teachers who have tried this (although they are often reluctant at first) soon report that they can pick up the pace and accomplish just as much with five minutes less.

Instead of independent reading, morning work and packing up time could also be allocated to teacher read-aloud. In one second-grade class, the teacher begins the day with teacher read-aloud and ends the day with independent reading time, demonstrating daily the importance of helping all students obtain the reading habit.

Teachers Use Both Fiction and Nonfiction as Read-Alouds

"My teacher read it aloud to us" is the most common response children give when asked why they chose a particular book to read. Children often want to read books that teachers read aloud to them—and probably other books on the same topic or by the same author. But what if the books a teacher is reading aloud are not a student's preferred type of book? Bookstores report that they sell 80 percent of their fiction to women and 80 percent of their informational books to men. When we first heard this statistic on NPR, we were shocked. Upon reflection, however, we realized that most of the reading Pat and her female friend share is fiction—John Grisham, Anne Tyler, and Jan Karon, to name a few. Most of the reading Jim and other men we know do is nonfiction—books about baseball and Civil War battles and biographies. After determining based on personal experience that the fiction/nonfiction preference is probably true, Pat began to worry about what teachers—those in elementary school are predominantly female—were reading to their students. She surveyed teachers in workshops, and, sure enough, the majority of what teachers read to their students is fiction. If males have a preference for reading informational books—books about spiders, or football, or Australia—they are less likely to want to read the fiction book the teacher has read aloud to them.

One simple change teachers can make that would go a long way toward motivating boys to read is to include equal amounts of fiction and nonfiction in daily teacher read-aloud. *Charlotte's Web* might be followed by Gail Gibbons' wonderfully illustrated book *Spiders*. Together, the fictional *Tonight on the Titanic* and the nonfictional *Titanic Research Guide* would provide a good balance of historical fiction and fact.

Another gender-based difference seems to be a preference by men for magazines over books. In classrooms that have subscriptions to *National Geographic Kids*, *Sports Illustrated Kids*, and *Zoobooks*, and in which teachers read aloud parts of these magazines when they arrive each month, all kids—both girls and boys—are clamoring to read for themselves what the teacher reads aloud.

Teachers Develop Meaning Vocabulary During Read-Alouds

Teacher read-aloud provides a major opportunity for children to learn new word meanings. Several studies have demonstrated the power of focused read-alouds on fostering vocabulary growth (Beck, McKeown, & Kucan, 2002; Juel et al., 2003). In each of these studies, the teachers went beyond just reading books aloud to children. Before they read a book aloud, they selected a few important words they felt many children would not know the meanings of. After the book had been read aloud and discussed, the teachers returned to those selected words and focused student attention on them.

Teacher read-aloud is the perfect opportunity to model how to use context, pictures, and word parts to figure out the meanings of words. Imagine that you are reading *Charlotte's Web* aloud to some third graders. Early in the book, Fern's dad plans to kill the little pig because he is a runt and a weakling. Fern pleads for his life and declares that killing the pig would be a terrible case of injustice. This is a perfect opportunity to model for students how to figure out what *injustice* means. Fern clearly feels that it is not fair to kill the pig just because he is little. *Justice* can mean *fairness*. When Fern argues that killing the pig would be an injustice, she is saying that it would be unfair.

Informational books present numerous opportunities to teach students how to use pictures to figure out what words mean. In the first pages of a book on deserts, for example, the meanings of words such as *mesa, butte, dune, canyon, cactus,* and *succulents* are built through the pictures and accompanying text.

Students Have Choice of and Access to a Wide Range of Materials

A child who does not like to read is simply a child who has not found the right book. Teachers who have the most successful independent reading programs have collected many different kinds of reading material and encourage children to choose. In addition to traditional books for their grade level, they provide informational books connected to the science and social studies themes being studied. Popular series books, such as the Junie B. Jones books, Cam Jansen mysteries, Captain Underpants books, and Harry Potter books are part of the classroom collection. There are joke and riddle books. Dr. Seuss and other beginning reader books are available, and children are encouraged to read them in class and then choose one to take home to read to a younger sibling, cousin, or neighbor.

In addition to books, these teachers have magazines—*Ranger Rick, American Girl, TIME For Kids,* and *Weekly Reader,* for example. Children can return to back issues of these magazines again and again.

Being able to choose what you want to read is crucial for developing the reading habit. If teachers indicate that their struggling readers are mostly boys who won't read during independent reading time, look at what is available for them to choose. If the classroom library is 90 percent fiction chapter books written at grade level or above, boys may have few choices that match both their ability and interest.

Resources for Teacher Read-Aloud and Independent Reading Study Groups

Making time for teacher read-aloud and independent reading provides many benefits that make a significant difference in the long term but are often difficult or impossible to measure in the short term. Principals should empower teachers to provide their students with these simple, pleasurable, and nourishing activities daily.

If improving your school's teacher read-aloud and independent reading practices is one of your priorities, see the reproducible list of resources on page 81. These resources provide detailed descriptions and lesson templates that will help your teachers overcome the roadblocks and implement the best practices described in this chapter. Articles from *The Reading Teacher* are included because they are quick reads that can launch your discussions and because they are accessible online with a subscription.

The State of Teacher Read-Aloud and Independent Reading in Your School

This chapter has answered three important questions about teacher read-aloud and independent reading: What misconceptions act as roadblocks in the way of implementing these activities? What do good teacher read-aloud and independent reading look like? What specific resources could you use to help your teachers improve their teacher read-aloud and independent reading?

Compared with other areas, teacher read-aloud and independent reading may be a relative weakness or strength in your school. To help you decide whether you need to intervene with some or all of your teachers with a study group or other professional development, we have compiled an informal checklist (page 82) for considering the state of teacher read-aloud and independent reading in your school. If you decide an intervention is needed in this area, you may find the same checklist useful to help you determine the effectiveness of the intervention.

Teacher Read-Aloud and Independent Reading Resources

The following books contain practical suggestions for getting all students to read and clever ways to expand classroom libraries:

- Layne, S. L. (2009). *Igniting a passion for reading: Successful strategies for building lifetime readers.* Portland, ME: Stenhouse.

- Moss, B., & Young, T. A. (2010). *Creating lifelong readers through independent reading.* Newark, DE: International Reading Association.

- Stead, T. (2009). *Good choice! Supporting independent reading and response, K–6.* Portland, ME: Stenhouse.

This book, written by a sixth-grade teacher, will inspire upper-grade teachers who might have given up on trying to get their older students to read:

- Miller, D. (2009). *The book whisperer: Awakening the inner reader in every child.* San Francisco: Jossey-Bass.

The following are some practical articles on teacher read-aloud and independent reading from *The Reading Teacher*:

- Fisher, D., Flood, J., Lapp, D., & Frey, N. (2004). Interactive read-alouds: Is there a common set of implementation practices? *The Reading Teacher, 58*(1), 8–17.

- Kelley, M., & Clausen-Grace, N. (2006). R^5: The sustained silent reading makeover that transformed readers. *The Reading Teacher, 64*(3), 191–195.

- Kelley, M. J., & Clausen-Grace, N. (2009). Facilitating engagement by differentiating independent reading. *The Reading Teacher, 63*(4), 313–318.

- Lane, H. B., & Wright, T. L. (2007). Maximizing the effectiveness of reading aloud. *The Reading Teacher, 60*(7), 668–675.

- Ranker, J. (2007). Using comic books as read-alouds: Insights on reading instruction from an English as a second language classroom. *The Reading Teacher, 61*(4), 296–305.

- Santoro, L. E., Chard, D. J., Howard, L., & Baker, S. K. (2008). Making the very most of classroom read-alouds to promote comprehension and vocabulary. *The Reading Teacher,* 61(5), 396–408.

Teacher Read-Aloud and Independent Reading: What to Look For

As you observe in classrooms and examine lesson plans and class schedules, ask the following questions about what you see, hear, and read:

1. Do teachers reserve time each day to read aloud and for independent reading?

    ☐ Frequently   ☐ Occasionally   ☐ Rarely   ☐ Never

    Comments:

2. Do teachers include both fiction and nonfiction in their read-alouds?

    ☐ Frequently   ☐ Occasionally   ☐ Rarely   ☐ Never

    Comments:

3. Do teachers seize opportunities to build word meanings during their read-alouds?

    ☐ Frequently   ☐ Occasionally   ☐ Rarely   ☐ Never

    Comments:

4. For independent reading, do students get to choose from a variety of reading materials?

    ☐ Frequently   ☐ Occasionally   ☐ Rarely   ☐ Never

    Comments:

EIGHT
READING MOTIVATION AND ENGAGEMENT

It is not enough for students to be in the presence of reading instruction appropriate to their needs; they must be engaged and cooperative—they must meet the teacher halfway. Likewise, when students read independently, it is not enough for them to sit quietly, move their eyes over the lines of print, and try to remember details; they must become cognitively and emotionally involved in the reading—whether real or make-believe. Motivation to read and to learn to read better is necessary for students—it's not just nice. The bad news is many students lack engagement with reading and reading instruction; however, the good news is there are proven ways to increase students' motivation in reading.

The Roadblocks to Reading Engagement

Before thinking about what can be done to increase student motivation and engagement in reading, we must think about why many students are turned off to reading. In our experience, there are three major roadblocks that hinder student motivation and engagement.

Assuming That Motivation Equals Excitement or Fun

We believe excitement and fun have a place in the literacy classroom. However, the idea that they are the heart of motivation ignores the research on the topic. Feelings play a part in engagement, but students' values and beliefs are generally more determinative of what they do and don't do (Gambrell, 2011).

Marzano and Pickering (2010) have posed commonsense questions corresponding to four different factors in student motivation identified by research:

1. How do I feel?

2. Am I interested?

3. Is it important?

4. Can I do it?

As we understand the body of research on reading engagement, these questions are probably ordered from least to most significant. The first two fit mostly in the affective domain; the last two are primarily cognitive.

The fourth one—Can I do it?—targets student self-efficacy. That is, it asks whether learners believe they will be successful before they engage in a particular activity or task. This belief will be based on a student's past experiences in similar situations and whether the student thinks he or she has the strategies and knowledge the activity or task seems to require. When students lack self-efficacy in reading, they are likely to resist engaging in reading or with reading instruction. If they do engage, they are likely to give up and quit as soon as the reading becomes challenging.

To motivate unmotivated students in reading, teachers can try to generate some excitement or fun. Teachers will accomplish more, however, if they help students realize the value of reading and gain confidence that they can succeed at it.

Assuming Students Know the Value of Reading

Marzano and Pickering's (2010) third question—Is it important?—should probably be reworded as "Is it important now?" Adults know how valuable reading well is for children's future schooling, career success, and quality of life. In the meantime, adults know those standardized accountability measures are coming! It is easy for teachers to project their values of reading and learning to read better onto students. The problem is that children are not adults. If reading does not seem important to them day to day, then most students will have great difficulty behaving as if it has much value.

As part of the 2005 NAEP Reading assessment (Perie et al., 2005), fourth graders were asked whether they believed they learned much from reading. Fifty-nine percent of them answered negatively. So, three out of five fourth graders did not consider reading important for learning. Seventy-three percent reported they did not read frequently for enjoyment. So, three out of four fourth graders did not consider reading important for quality of life. We have no reason to think these student attitudes have improved since 2005.

The majority of students need convincing that reading has value for them personally, but speeches during which adults share how important it is to us and ought to be to them cannot accomplish that. Instead, the nation's foremost authority on reading engagement, John Guthrie (2011), has written that the best way is to "attempt to situate the benefit of literacy in a concrete situation" (p. 190). One procedure he recommends is straightforward. The teacher shows students a video clip on a topic in science or social studies and then reads an interesting, informative, and short text on the same topic. After reading, the students are paired and share the new things they have learned, jotting them down on a piece of scratch paper. The teacher then leads a class discussion on the question, "What were your sources of new learning today?" (p. 190). At first, many students will say they learned most from the video or their partner, but eventually they will come to see that, in fact, reading is the best source of new learning on a topic. Repeating this kind of exercise over time can go a long way to convincing students they can learn from reading.

In the previous chapter, we showed that independent reading and teacher read-aloud done well teach students the value of reading for enjoyment and social interaction. After all, that's why we do those activities—not only to help children read better, but also to assist them in becoming lifelong readers for all the benefits they will accrue from it.

Providing Extrinsic Points or Prizes for Reading

Marzano and Pickering's (2010) four questions all focus on intrinsic motivation—reading for reasons internal to the student. However, anyone who has spent much time in schools knows that the most common methods of increasing engagement rely on a particular kind of extrinsic motivation: rewarding individual students with tokens of some kind for reading or learning to read better.

What difference does it make? If they read more or better, does it matter how the teacher got them to do it? As it turns out, it does. However we attempt to achieve it, increased intrinsic motivation must be the goal. If students are only motivated extrinsically, they will not engage in reading or reading tasks when there is no one around to reward them. Consequently, they will not read outside of school in the evenings, on weekends, during school holidays, or over summer vacations. We will have won a battle, perhaps, but lost the war.

In the 1970s, researchers began to distinguish between intrinsic and extrinsic motivation. Later, they distinguished between two kinds of extrinsic motivators: tangible and intangible. Relative to this roadblock, the results of decades of research are in: the use of tangible extrinsic motivators fails to build intrinsic motivation and actually destroys it in those who already have it. In the classic study, Lepper, Greene, and Nisbett (1973) used a one-way mirror to identify young children who spontaneously chose to draw during free time. They rewarded some of them with tokens for drawing. After they stopped rewarding them, those children no longer chose to engage in drawing during free time as they had done before the experiment. Similar studies have been done since then, leading one researcher to conclude that tangible rewards reduce rather than build intrinsic motivation (Deci, 1992).

Of course, it is easier to change student behavior short-term using tangible rewards such as stickers than to build intrinsic motivation. However, what matters in the medium and long terms is to help students learn to answer "Yes" to each of Marzano and Pickering's (2010) four questions, especially the last two.

Best Practices for Reading Engagement and Motivation

To determine how well your school is producing engaged readers, look at how teachers are attempting to motivate students and what best practices they use. Observe whether or not they are unintentionally undermining student motivation.

Teachers Maintain a Supportive, Nurturing Classroom Environment

As valuable as specific strategies for building student motivation in reading can be, they exist within a larger context. The ongoing emotional climate of the classroom must be such that particular attempts to increase reading engagement are consistent with it, not in opposition to it. Jim cannot forget the classroom he visited early in his career where a teacher noticed a child off-task and called loudly across the room to a busy child who was working nearby—and with an amazing amount of venom and anger in her voice—"Thank you for working." No set of strategies for motivating children can possibly overcome a negative atmosphere like that classroom had.

As stated in chapter 1, effective reading instruction requires a supportive, nurturing classroom environment. Caring, positive, respectful classrooms where teachers take student interests into account when planning activities provide the right context within which specific approaches to increase reading engagement can succeed.

Students Get No Tangible Rewards Except Those Linked to Reading

The obvious advantage of giving out tokens is that they are quick and simple to administer when students are doing what we like. We don't have to change how or what we're teaching to get additional cooperation from learners. What happens, though, during standardized testing when giving out tokens is forbidden? What happens if next year's teacher does not choose to use tangible rewards? In these cases and others, the lack of intrinsic motivation will soon manifest itself to no one's benefit. Helping teachers replace pizzas, points, or prizes with other means of building reading engagement is the purpose of the rest of this chapter.

There is only one kind of tangible reward that has been shown to build rather than destroy readers' intrinsic motivation. Gambrell (2011) has investigated proximal rewards, those directly linked to reading, and discovered that they, unlike other tangible rewards, can be effective in developing intrinsic motivation. Specifically, such rewards consist of "books, bookmarks, extra time for pleasure reading, and extra teacher read-aloud time" (p. 56).

If teachers are strongly wedded to giving out tangible rewards in reading, helping them to change their rewards from pizzas, points, or prizes to those that are linked to reading itself can maintain short-term student engagement while significantly reducing the harmful effects nonreading-related rewards have on intrinsic motivation. If teachers believe such rewards would not motivate their students, suggest that they try the strategy for at least a couple of weeks.

Students Have Mini-Choices

According to Guthrie (2011), "The most widespread recommendation for motivation is providing choices" (p. 187). Students don't need unlimited choices but rather a moderate amount of managed or limited choice. Guthrie, himself, is an advocate of what he calls "mini-choices" (p. 188). For example, in chapter 2 on comprehension, we suggested that primary teachers regularly ask students after reading to choose their favorite part or decide what the most interesting new fact was that they learned. Note that, in this case, the teacher chooses what the students will read and how the lesson will proceed, but that doesn't mean the students have no choices to make.

Possible mini-choices include writing questions to ask a partner, small group, or the class after reading; choosing which five out of ten questions the student will answer; selecting which paragraph or page to read aloud; selecting which book to read independently; in a K-W-L, choosing two or three Ws to read to find out; and so on. Students shouldn't be allowed to run the classroom, determine the curriculum, or veto instructional strategies so they have choices that motivate them and develop ownership over their learning. Moreover, giving students *many* mini-choices over time can help them develop autonomy as learners (Guthrie, 2011), which they must have to succeed in middle and high school, when both teacher and parental supervision is significantly reduced.

Teachers Include Strategy Lessons to Increase Student Success

Arguably, lack of self-efficacy is the biggest motivational problem our students have. Of course, that tends to be true for all those who struggle in reading, but it is also true for those who have been reasonably successful but are either sensitive to criticism or perfectionists. Anyone who has had children knows how fragile their self-confidence can be.

Research has shown where we must concentrate efforts if we are to build student self-efficacy in reading: we must teach students *how* to be more successful. Schunk and Zimmerman (1997) found that failures by themselves do not destroy self-efficacy as long as learners blame the approach they took rather than themselves. They also found that when students are taught a strategy for how to complete a task successfully, it significantly increases their sense of efficacy for that kind of task. This is why it is so important for teachers to prepare students adequately before giving them an assignment to complete either in the classroom or for homework.

Another important finding of the Schunk and Zimmerman study was that teacher praise and positive feedback that are honest also increase student self-efficacy. This was especially true in comprehension and writing where students often have trouble evaluating their own performance and growth. However, praise and positive feedback do not help when students still experience failure.

Finally, they discovered that the right kind of modeling builds self-efficacy. What they call "coping models," are more effective than "mastery models." That is, when a teacher or student reads or performs a task after reading while thinking out loud, it builds self-efficacy better for those watching when the model has (or pretends to have) and overcomes difficulty than when the model reads or performs the task flawlessly. In other words, what must be modeled is the use of one or more strategies to succeed where otherwise one would fail, rather than a situation where no strategy is needed.

Unfortunately, it is not sufficient to build students' self-efficacy by teaching and modeling strategies; teachers must also avoid practices that undermine self-efficacy. A diet of texts and tasks that are too hard for a student to succeed at regardless of effort will eventually reduce self-efficacy (Schunk & Zimmerman, 1997). Perhaps most importantly, teachers must make sure students are not scolded or otherwise made to feel badly because of mistakes made or wrong answers. Receiving such responses leads to students devaluing academic work and eventually developing an "I don't care" attitude toward it (Strambler & Weinstein, 2010).

Resources for Motivation Study Groups

Students who are engaged and motivated learn more than children who are simply waiting for lunch or recess. If improving motivation and engagement in your school is one of your priorities, see the reproducible resources list on page 89. These resources will help your teachers overcome the roadblocks and implement the best practices described in this chapter. Articles from *The Reading Teacher* are included because they are quick reads that can launch your discussions and because they are accessible online with a subscription.

The State of Reading Motivation and Engagement in Your School

This chapter has answered three important questions about reading motivation and engagement: What misconceptions act as roadblocks in the way of achieving higher levels of reading motivation and engagement? What do good reading motivation and engagement look like? What specific resources could you use to help your teachers build reading motivation and engagement?

Compared with other areas of reading, reading motivation and engagement may be a relative weakness or strength in your school. To help you decide whether you need to intervene with some or all of your teachers with a study group or other professional development, we have compiled an informal checklist (page 90) for considering the state of reading motivation and engagement in your school. If you decide an intervention is needed in reading motivation and engagement, you may find the same checklist useful to help you determine the effectiveness of the intervention.

Reading Motivation and Engagement Resources

Motivating students to read and to learn to read better is necessary. The following books contain excellent suggestions for building reading engagement:

- Marinak, B. A., Gambrell, L. B., & Mazzoni, S. A. (2012). *Maximizing motivation for literacy learning: Grades K–6*. New York: Guilford Press.
- Marzano, R. J., & Pickering, D. J. (2010). *The highly engaged classroom*. Bloomington, IN: Marzano Research Laboratory.
- Schreck, M. K. (2011). *You've got to reach them to teach them: Hard facts about the soft skills of student engagement*. Bloomington, IN: Solution Tree Press.

The following are practical articles on reading engagement from *The Reading Teacher*:

- Applegate, A. J., & Applegate, M. D. (2010). A study of thoughtful literacy and the motivation to read. *The Reading Teacher, 64*(4), 226–234.
- Edmunds, K. M., & Bauserman, K. L. (2006). What teachers can learn about reading motivation through conversations with children. *The Reading Teacher, 59*(5), 414–424.
- Gambrell, L. (2011). Seven rules of engagement. *The Reading Teacher, 65*(3), 204–208.

Reading Motivation and Engagement: What to Look For

As you observe in classrooms and examine lesson plans and class schedules, ask the following questions about what you see, hear, and read:

1. Do teachers maintain a supportive, nurturing classroom environment?

   ☐ Frequently ☐ Occasionally ☐ Rarely ☐ Never

   Comments:

2. Do teachers avoid using tangible rewards for reading (except those directly linked to reading)?

   ☐ Frequently ☐ Occasionally ☐ Rarely ☐ Never

   Comments:

3. Do teachers allow students to make mini-choices?

   ☐ Frequently ☐ Occasionally ☐ Rarely ☐ Never

   Comments:

4. When students are having difficulty, do teachers teach them a strategy so they can succeed?

   ☐ Frequently ☐ Occasionally ☐ Rarely ☐ Never

   Comments:

NINE

STRUGGLING READERS AND ENGLISH LEARNERS

In every school there are children for whom learning to read is an unusually difficult task. Starting in the mid sixties, federal and local money has been spent providing a variety of remedial services for these students. Struggling readers have been pulled out for thirty-minute sessions with Title I reading teachers or aides. Children diagnosed as learning disabled have been given reading instruction consistent with their individual education plan. Many children who are behind in reading are English learners simultaneously acquiring a new language and learning to read in it. Millions of dollars are spent each year on these remedial efforts, but there is very little evidence that any of these programs are generally effective. Most children who are behind in reading in first grade are further behind by the time they leave elementary school, in spite of their participation in a variety of remedial programs.

The Roadblocks to Supporting Struggling Readers and English Learners

Why are these reading problems so intransigent? Why did one-third of fourth graders who took the NAEP Reading test in 2009 fail to score even at the basic level and only one-third of fourth graders score at proficient or advanced levels? With little to show for all the time, effort, and money expended on struggling readers, we must reevaluate what we are doing and consider how we might provide instruction that would actually move children forward and begin to close achievement gaps. There are common roadblocks to supporting learners that are not easy to get beyond.

Extra Instruction Is Not Really Extra

Historically, the "extra" reading instruction students having difficulty received was given instead of rather than in addition to classroom instruction. Students went down the hall to the reading room or the special education room and returned to their classrooms thirty to forty minutes later, and everyone assumed they received the reading instruction they needed. The belief that 30 or 40 minutes of small-group instruction are sufficient to move struggling read-ers forward is a major roadblock. As we noted in chapter 1, reading is complex. In addition to learning phonics, children must learn to track print, develop fluency, increase the size of their meaning vocabularies, and learn comprehension strategies for both fiction and informational texts. That complexity is the reason teachers need uninterrupted literacy blocks—120 minutes in primary grades and 90 minutes in upper grades. If children who are not struggling with learning to read need 90 to 120 minutes of comprehensive literacy instruction each day, how can we possibly expect children who struggle with reading to make any progress with only 30 to 40 minutes?

The recognition that children who struggle with reading need more—not less—instruction is one of the main contributions of the RTI initiative passed as part of the Individuals with Disabilities Education Improvement Act (IDEA) in 2004. RTI changes the way children are classified as learning disabled. Prior to RTI, the decision that a child had a learning disability in reading was made by looking at the discrepancy between the child's potential as measured by an IQ test and the child's reading achievement. The theory was that if a child had aver-age or above average intelligence and was below average in reading, that child must have some brain-related disability that was keeping him or her from achieving. Many of us who have worked with children labeled "learning disabled" believed that some of them were more "teaching disabled." They had not experienced a strong multidimensional reading instructional program in their classrooms.

The essence of RTI lies in its three tiers of instruction. Tier 1 is defined as high-quality classroom instruction with regular progress monitoring. The purpose of Tier 1 is to ensure children have had multiple opportunities to learn in the classroom setting and that how well they are progressing with that instruction is being assessed. Tier 2 consists of interventions designed for children who are not making adequate progress in spite of receiving high-quality classroom instruction. Tier 2 instruction is generally done in small groups of three to five stu-dents provided by the classroom teacher or by a specialist. RTI specifies that Tier 2 instruction be in addition to—not instead of—regular classroom instruction. If your school has an effective RTI program, children who struggle with reading receive high-quality instruction in their classrooms plus *extra* reading instruction in a small-group setting.

Progress in Tier 2 is closely monitored. Children who do not make adequate progress in Tier 2 instruction are referred for special education services and are often classified as learn-ing disabled. Intensive interventions and monitoring are provided for these children in Tier 3.

One-Size-Fits-All Tier 2 Instruction

In chapter 5, we shared results from several studies indicating that intermediate elemen-tary and middle school students who struggle with reading often have strengths in phonics and fluency as compared to their comprehension and meaning vocabulary. RTI specifies that Tier 2 instruction should be targeted toward the specific reading needs of students. In a synthesis of twenty-four studies of fourth- and fifth-grade struggling readers, the researchers concluded that there were high effects for comprehension-oriented interventions and low to moderate effects for word-recognition interventions (Wanzek, Wexler, Vaughn, & Ciullo, 2010). In syntheses of studies with students in grades six to twelve, researchers found large effects for vocabulary interventions and moderate effects for multi-component interventions (Edmonds et al., 2009; Kamil et al., 2008; Scammacca et al., 2007).

We have also witnessed the success of targeting interventions toward specific needs of students in reading. The RTI program in several elementary and middle schools in Orange and Durham Counties, North Carolina, follows a diagnostic model and assigns students to groups according to their area of greatest need in reading (Erickson, 2011). Students who need Tier 2 instruction are given informal reading inventories to assess them on silent reading comprehension, listening comprehension, and word identification in order to generate a profile of three scores for each individual. Each profile is then interpreted to determine in which of three areas a student most needs instruction now to grow in reading. Intervention groups are then formed to address each area of need. Some teachers instruct groups composed of students whose weakness is language comprehension, while other teachers instruct groups of students who need work in word identification, while still other teachers instruct groups of students whose weakness is print processing beyond word identification. Periodically, the informal reading inventories are re-administered and, if their area of greatest need has changed, students are reassigned to the appropriate group.

In chapter 1, we described how assessment can promote or hinder good instruction. Teachers cannot provide targeted interventions to students if they don't know which component of reading is causing students the most difficulty. Diagnostic assessments can provide us with the information needed to determine what kind of instruction students need most at a point in time and adjust that instruction as needs change.

The Belief That Some Children Will Never Be Good Readers

In the previous chapter, we expressed how important self-efficacy is to student engagement and motivation. Students who believe they can do something will put forth the effort needed to achieve it. Repeated failure with reading tasks convinces many students that reading is just not something they will ever be good at.

Self-efficacy is important for teachers, too. If teachers see children fail to learn in spite of their best efforts, and if the children they send down the hall to the "experts" still don't make progress in reading, it is reasonable for them to assume that some children are just never going to read well. The failure of Reading First affected children and also undermined the self-efficacy of many teachers who diligently implemented the scripted programs they were given and failed to see the success those programs promised or receive the accolades they had been led to expect. Improving the quality of the literacy instruction in your school will become a self-fulfilling prophecy. Teachers will come to believe that children make reading progress when they are given excellent and multidimensional classroom instruction in a supportive emotional environment. Students who need more than that will also progress if their extra instruction is truly extra and targeted to their needs. Seeing really *is* believing!

Best Practices for Supporting Struggling Readers and English Learners

Many schools have a variety of beyond-the-classroom supports in place for children who struggle with reading. Describing all the different features of the many remedial programs in place is way beyond the scope of this book, but here are a few big items you should consider in evaluating your school's support for struggling readers.

Struggling Readers and English Learners Get Extra Support

The first thing to evaluate is whether the extra instruction struggling readers get is truly in addition to and not instead of good classroom instruction. To determine this, look at when students are getting additional instruction and what they are missing in their classrooms. If students are being pulled out of their classrooms during the classroom literacy block, the instruction they are getting is not extra. Struggling readers are not getting any additional minutes of instruction. Recognizing this problem is easy. Figuring out how to solve it requires some creative scheduling. Here are some scheduling ideas clever administrators have devised.

In some schools, children who need additional literacy instruction receive that instruction before the school day begins or as part of after-school activities. The workday for specials teachers begins an hour earlier or an hour later than it does for classroom teachers, and these teachers go home an hour earlier or an hour later. Children who need extra instruction and who can arrive at school earlier or stay later receive that instruction and can participate fully in their classroom instruction. This solution won't work for every school or for all the children within a school. If almost all children ride buses, the buses arrive just in time for the school day, and there is no after-school program, then there is no time for before- or after-school interventions. In most schools, however, some children can come to school early, and some children remain in the building after school. Providing additional literacy instruction for those children outside the normal school hours does not solve the problem for everyone, but it does provide a solution for some.

Another approach some schools take is to schedule additional literacy instruction during social studies or science time. The teacher providing that instruction teaches the same social studies or science content; the difference is that he or she focuses on developing literacy skills using social studies or science materials.

In one school, the English as a second language teacher pulls students out during their social studies time. She uses the social studies text but scaffolds their learning so that they can learn the content and improve their reading and writing skills. Each lesson begins with the teacher and students previewing the text section to be read and learning all they can from the illustrations, charts, graphs, maps, and diagrams—visuals that are common to all social studies texts. Next, she introduces key vocabulary, helping children pronounce the words and associate meaning with them and using the visuals to scaffold many of the word meanings. Then the teacher reads the text to the students, stopping after each paragraph to help them summarize what they have learned. The final activity is a shared writing activity during which the students and teacher compose a summary of what they learned. The next class period begins with students reviewing what they learned from the visuals and reading together the summary they composed before they move to that day's section. Children are given a typed copy of each day's summary to which they add an illustration and then put it in their social studies notebook.

In addition to solving the "extra, not instead of" problem in reading, combining science or social studies content with literacy instruction has additional benefits. In chapter 3, we described the importance of meaning vocabulary knowledge to comprehension and the need for students to be adding 1,000 to 2,000 new word meanings to their vocabulary stores each year. One of the things you evaluated was whether teachers in your school are focusing on vocabulary while teaching math, science, and social studies. Teachers who use science or social studies content as the basis for their instruction with struggling readers or English learners have the opportunity to focus on building academic vocabulary with the very children who are most in need of vocabulary development. They can also focus on the special comprehension skills needed to understand informational text.

One other way to make sure the instruction students are receiving is adding to reading instruction is to schedule a block of time in every classroom for enrichment and remediation. In some schools, each grade level has a thirty-minute block of time during which all students are involved in enrichment or remediation activities. All teachers at that grade level and specials teachers—including media specialists—work with students on a variety of activities, including literacy and math remediation.

Providing instruction that is extra and not just a replacement for classroom literacy instruction is not easy. Administrators must think outside the box and be open to creative scheduling to make sure struggling students receive the extra instruction they need.

Instruction Is Tailored to Student Needs

Regardless of what kind of extra instruction students are getting, for it to be effective, that instruction must be targeted to their specific needs. Targeting specific needs is one of the requirements of RTI and is the reason IEPs are developed for children in special education programs. With the current emphasis on phonics, many schools have adopted a remedial phonics program. Using a phonics program with all children who are having difficulty learning to read assumes that phonics is the area of greatest need for all struggling students. In chapter 5, we summarized research that concluded that many older students who are not achieving in reading have strengths in word identification when compared with their comprehension and vocabulary skills. We personally have found that to be the case to a lesser degree in second and third grade as well. Earlier in this chapter, we cited research summaries demonstrating that older students made more progress when their interventions had a comprehension, vocabulary, or multicomponent focus. Examine the instruction your struggling readers are receiving. If everyone is getting more or less the same program, and if that program is narrowly focused on phonemic awareness, phonics, and fluency, you must help teachers incorporate some assessment measures that determine each student's area of greatest need. Some of the students will need a continued emphasis on word identification, but many others will need different instruction if they are to become better readers.

Struggling readers and English learners need targeted Tier 2 instruction that is truly extra. Often, this combination of targeted and extra instruction will be enough. While a few students will need Tier 3 instruction that is really different than anything they've previously had, most students who are behind just need more targeted instruction to catch up.

Teachers Believe All Children Can Learn to Read

Self-efficacy, the belief that you can accomplish something if you work at it, is as critical for teachers as it is for children. No one is going to admit they don't believe all children can learn to read. However, if teachers have been putting forth their best efforts and not seeing results, it is understandable they will conclude that some children are just not going to ever become proficient readers. Just as with children, pep talks and lectures will do little to convince teachers that "you can really do it if you try." Supporting teachers with the time and knowledge to provide high-quality, multifaceted literacy instruction and making sure struggling readers and English learners get extra and targeted instruction will result in them making measurable, observable progress. Once teachers see students beginning to make progress, they will come to believe their efforts are paying off and redouble those efforts. As the saying goes, "Nothing succeeds like success!"

Resources for Supporting Struggling Readers and English Learners

If one of your priorities is providing support for your struggling readers that is truly extra and targeted, see the reproducible resources list on page 98. These resources will help your teachers overcome the roadblocks and implement the best practices described in this chapter. Articles from *The Reading Teacher* are included because they are quick reads that can launch your discussions and because they are accessible online with a subscription.

The State of Your School's Support for Struggling Readers and English Learners

This chapter has answered three important questions about support for struggling readers and English learners: What misconceptions act as roadblocks in the way of providing optimal support? What does that optimal support look like? What specific resources could you use to help your teachers improve the support struggling readers and English learners receive?

Compared with other areas, the support for struggling readers and English learners may be a relative weakness or strength in your school. To help you decide whether you need to intervene with some or all of your teachers with a study group or other professional development, we have compiled an informal checklist (page 99) for considering the state of your school's support for struggling readers and English learners. If you decide an intervention is needed in this area, you may find the same checklist useful to help you determine the effectiveness of the intervention.

Struggling Reader and English Learner Resources

The following books contain practical suggestions for implementing successful classroom programs and interventions for struggling readers:

- Allington, R. L. (2012). *What really matters for struggling readers: Designing research-based programs* (3rd ed.). Boston: Pearson.

- Cunningham, P. M., & Allington, R. L. (2011). *Classrooms that work: They can all read and write* (5th ed.). Boston: Pearson.

- Paratore, J. R., & McCormack, R. L. (2011). *After early intervention, then what? Teaching struggling readers in grades 3 and beyond* (2nd ed.). Newark, DE: International Reading Association.

These books are excellent resources for helping teachers tailor instruction for English learners:

- Bowers, E., & Keisler, L. (2012). *Building academic language through content-area text: Strategies to support English language learners.* Huntington Beach, CA: Shell Education.

- Fisher, D., Frey, N., & Rothenberg, C. (2011). *Implementing RTI with English learners.* Bloomington, IN: Solution Tree Press.

- Mora-Flores, E. (2011). *Connecting content and language for English language learners.* Huntington Beach, CA: Shell Education.

The following are practical articles on English learners and struggling readers from *The Reading Teacher*:

- Bluestein, N. A. (2010). Unlocking text features for determining importance in expository text: A strategy for struggling readers. *The Reading Teacher, 63*(7), 597–600.

- Lipson, M. (2011). Diagnosis: The missing ingredient in RTI assessment. *The Reading Teacher, 65*(3), 204–208.

- Ogle, D., & Correa-Kovtun, A. (2010). Supporting English-language learners and struggling readers in content literacy with the "partner reading and content, too" routine. *The Reading Teacher, 63*(7), 532–542.

- Teale, W. H. (2009). Urban literacy: Students learning English and their literacy instruction in urban schools. *The Reading Teacher, 62*(8), 699–703.

Support for Struggling Readers and English Learners: What to Look For

As you observe in classrooms and examine lesson plans and class schedules, ask the following questions about what you see, hear, and read:

1. Is the support for struggling readers and English learners in addition to (rather than in place of) good classroom instruction?

   ☐ Frequently   ☐ Occasionally   ☐ Rarely   ☐ Never

   Comments:

2. Is the extra instruction struggling readers and English learners receive tailored to their needs?

   ☐ Frequently   ☐ Occasionally   ☐ Rarely   ☐ Never

   Comments:

3. Do teachers appear to believe that struggling readers and English learners can become good readers?

   ☐ Frequently   ☐ Occasionally   ☐ Rarely   ☐ Never

   Comments:

AFTERWORD

Our goal in writing this book has been to help you recognize roadblocks, determine the state of reading instruction in your school, and have a list of practical resources your teachers can use in study groups to upgrade their teaching in the areas of reading where your school most needs improvement. There is "no quick fix" for a school's reading program (Allington & Walmsley, 1995), but you can achieve steady progress with effort and teamwork. Nothing builds the morale of principals and teachers like the sense that we are all in this together and things are getting better for our students. Over the years, we have been blessed to witness the enthusiasm and gratification that professionals experience when they are doing a better job of teaching reading to all their students. We are excited at the prospect that this will happen in your school, and we can only hope that this book will help you reach that worthwhile goal!

REFERENCES

Allington, R. L., & Cunningham, P. M. (2007). *Schools that work: Where all children read and write*. Boston: Allyn & Bacon.

Allington, R. L., & Johnston, P. H. (2002). *Reading to learn: Lessons from exemplary fourth-grade classrooms*. New York: Guilford Press.

Allington, R. L., & Walmsley, S. A. (1995). *No quick fix: Rethinking literacy programs in America's elementary schools*. New York: Teachers College Press.

Anderson, L. W., Krathwohl, D. R., Airasian, P. W., Cruikshank, K. A., Mayer, R. E., Pintrich, P. R., et al. (2001). *A taxonomy for learning, teaching, and assessing: A revision of Bloom's taxonomy of educational objectives*. New York: Longman.

Anderson, R. C., Wilson, P. T., & Fielding, L. G. (1988). Growth in reading and how children spend their time outside of school. *Reading Research Quarterly, 23*, 285–303.

Artley, S. A. (1975). Good teachers of reading—Who are they? *The Reading Teacher, 29*, 26–31.

Bangert-Drowns, R. L., Hurley, M. M., & Wilkinson, B. (2004). The effects of school-based writing-to-learn interventions on academic achievement: A meta-analysis. *Review of Educational Research, 74*, 29–58.

Baumann, J. F., Kame'enui, E. J., & Ash, G. E. (2003). Research on vocabulary instruction: Voltaire redux. In J. Flood, D. Lapp, J. R. Squire, & J. M. Jensen (Eds.), *Handbook of research on teaching the English language arts* (2nd ed., pp. 752–785). Mahwah, NJ: Erlbaum.

Becker, W. C. (1977). Teaching reading and language to the disadvantaged: What we have learned from field research. *Harvard Educational Review, 47*(4), 518–543.

Beck, I. L., McKeown, M. G., & Gromoll, E. W. (1989). Learning from social studies texts. *Cognition and Instruction, 6*(2), 99–158.

Beck, I. L., McKeown, M. G., & Kucan, L. (2002). *Bringing words to life: Robust vocabulary instruction*. New York: Guilford Press.

Benjamin, B. (2006). *Will Ron fix his rig?* (Storytown Reader #8). Orlando, FL: Harcourt School.

Biemiller, A. (2004). Teaching vocabulary in the primary grades. In J. F. Baumann & E. J. Kame'enui (Eds.), *Vocabulary instruction: Research to practice* (pp. 28–40). New York: Guilford Press.

Biemiller, A., & Slonim, M. (2001). Estimating root word vocabulary growth in normative and advantaged populations: Evidence for a common sequence of vocabulary acquisition. *Journal of Educational Psychology, 93*(3), 498–520.

Blachowicz, C. L. Z., & Fisher, P. (2000). Vocabulary instruction. In M. L. Kamil, P. B. Mosenthal, P. D. Pearson, & R. Barr (Eds.), *Handbook of reading research* (Vol. 3, pp. 503–523). Mahwah, NJ: Erlbaum.

Bloom, B. S., Engelhart, M. D., Furst, E. J., Hill, W. H., & Krathwohl, D. R. (1956). *Taxonomy of educational objectives: The classification of educational goals; Handbook I: Cognitive domain.* New York: Longman.

Bryk, A. S., & Schneider, B. (2002). *Trust in schools: A core resource for improvement.* New York: SAGE Foundation.

Buly, M., & Valencia, S. W. (2002). Below the bar: Profiles of students who fail state reading assessment. *Educational Evaluation and Policy Analysis, 24*(3), 219–239.

Coleman, D., & Pimentel, S. (2012a). *Publishers' criteria for the Common Core State Standards in English language arts and literacy, grades K–2.* Accessed at www.corestandards.org/assets/Publishers_Criteria_for_K-2.pdf on May 31, 2012.

Coleman, D., & Pimentel, S. (2012b). *Publishers' criteria for the Common Core State Standards in English language arts and literacy, grades 3–12.* Accessed at www.corestandards.org/assets /Publishers_Criteria_for_3-12.pdf on May 31, 2012.

Cunningham, A. E., & Stanovich, K. E. (1998). What reading does for the mind. *American Educator, 22*(1–2), 8–15.

Cunningham, J. W. (2001). Essay book review: The National Reading Panel report. *Reading Research Quarterly, 36*(3), 326–335.

Curran, S. (2006). *Pal has ham* (Storytown Reader #1). Orlando, FL: Harcourt School.

Deci, E. L. (1992). The relation of interest to the motivation of behavior: A self-determination theory perspective. In K. A. Renninger, S. Hidi, & A. Krapp (Eds.), *The role of interest in learning and development* (pp. 43–70). Hillsdale, NJ: Erlbaum.

Duke, N. K. (2010). The real-world reading and writing U.S. children need. *Phi Delta Kappan, 91*(5), 68–71.

Durkin, D. (1979). What classroom observations reveal about reading comprehension instruction. *Reading Research Quarterly, 14*(4), 481–533.

Edmonds, M. S., Vaughn, S., Wexler, J., Reutebuch, C., Cable, A., Tackett, K. K., et al. (2009). A synthesis of reading interventions and effects on reading comprehension outcomes for older struggling readers. *Review of Educational Research, 79*, 262–300.

Ehri, L. C., & Nunes, S. R. (2002). The role of phonemic awareness in learning to read. In A. E. Farstrup & S. J. Samuels (Eds.), *What research has to say about reading instruction* (3rd ed., pp. 110–139). Newark, DE: International Reading Association.

Erickson, K. A. (2011, November 30). *A theory-driven response to intervention approach.* Paper presented at the 2011 Literacy Research Association 61st Annual Conference, Jacksonville, FL.

Fisher, D., Frey, N., & Nelson, J. (2012). Literacy achievement through sustained professional development. *The Reading Teacher, 65*(8), 551–563.

Flesch, R. (1955). *Why Johnny can't read—and what you can do about it* (1st ed.). New York: Harper.

Foorman, B. R., & Connor, C. M. (2011). Primary grade reading. In M. L. Kamil, P. D. Pearson, E. B. Moje, & P. P. Afflerbach (Eds.), *Handbook of reading research* (Vol. 4, pp. 136–156). New York: Routledge.

Gambrell, L. B. (2011). Motivation in the school reading curriculum. In T. V. Rasinski (Ed.), *Rebuilding the foundation: Effective reading instruction for 21st century literacy* (pp. 41–65). Bloomington, IN: Solution Tree Press.

Gamse, B. C., Jacob, R. T., Horst, M., Boulay, B., & Unlu, F. (2008). *Reading First impact study: Final report* (NCEE 2009-4038). Washington, DC: National Center for Education Evaluation and Regional Assistance, Institute of Education Sciences, U.S. Department of Education.

Goddard, R. D., Tschannen-Moran, M., & Hoy, W. K. (2001). Teacher trust in students and parents: A multilevel examination of the distribution and effects of teacher trust in urban elementary schools. *Elementary School Journal, 102*, 3–17.

Goldman, S. R., & Rakestraw, J. A., Jr. (2000). Structural aspects of constructing meaning from text. In M. L. Kamil, P. B. Mosenthal, P. D. Pearson, & R. Barr (Eds.), *Handbook of reading research* (Vol. 3, pp. 311–335). Mahwah, NJ: Erlbaum.

Good, R. H., & Kaminski, R. A. (Eds.). (2002). *Dynamic Indicators of Basis Early Literacy Skills* (6th ed.). Eugene, OR: Institute for Development of Educational Achievement.

Graham, S., & Perin, D. (2007). A meta-analysis of writing instruction for adolescent students. *Journal of Educational Psychology, 99*(3), 445–476.

Graves, M. F. (2006). *The vocabulary book: Learning & instruction.* Newark, DE: International Reading Association.

Graves, M. F., & Watts-Taffe, S. M. (2002). The place of word consciousness in a research-based vocabulary program. In A. E. Farstrup & S. J. Samuels (Eds.), *What research has to say about reading instruction* (3rd ed., pp. 140–165). Newark, DE: International Reading Association.

Guthrie, J. T. (2011). Best practices in motivating students to read. In L. M. Morrow & L. B. Gambrell (Eds.), *Best practices in literacy instruction* (4th ed., pp. 177–198). New York: Guilford Press.

Guthrie, J. T., & Humenick, N. M. (2004). Motivating students to read: Evidence for classroom practices that increase motivation and achievement. In P. McCardle & V. Chhabra (Eds.), *The voice of evidence in reading research* (pp. 329–354). Baltimore: Brookes.

Guthrie, J. T., Wigfield, A., Humenick, N. M., Perencevich, K. C., Taboada, A., & Barbosa, P. (2006). Influences of stimulating tasks on reading motivation and comprehension. *Journal of Educational Research, 99*(4), 232–245.

Hamre, B. K., & Pianta, R. C. (2005). Can instructional and emotional support in the first-grade classroom make a difference for children at risk of school failure? *Child Development, 76*(5), 949–967.

Hart, B., & Risley, T. R. (1995). *Meaningful differences in the everyday experience of young American children.* Baltimore: Brookes.

Hedrick, W. B., & Cunningham, J. W. (2002). Investigating the effect of wide reading on listening comprehension of written language. *Reading Psychology, 23*(2), 107–126.

Hemphill, F. C., & Vanneman, A. (2010). *Achievement gaps: How Hispanic and white students in public schools perform in mathematics and reading on the National Assessment of Educational Progress* (NCES 2011-459). Washington, DC: National Center for Education Statistics, Institute of Education Sciences, U.S. Department of Education.

Herber, H. L. (1970). *Teaching reading in the content areas.* Englewood Cliffs, NJ: Prentice Hall.

Individuals with Disabilities Education Act, 20 U.S.C. § 1400 (2004).

Ivey, G., & Broaddus, K. (2001). "Just plain reading": A survey of what makes students want to read in middle school classrooms. *Reading Research Quarterly, 36*(4), 350–377.

Jackson, R., McCoy, A., Pistorino, C., Wilkinson, A., Burghardt, J., Clark, M., et al. (2007). *National evaluation of Early Reading First: Final report to Congress* (NCEE 2007-4007). Washington, DC: U.S. Department of Education, Institute of Education Sciences.

Juel, C., Biancarosa, G., Coker, D., & Deffes, R. (2003). Walking with Rosie: A cautionary tale of early reading instruction. *Educational Leadership, 60*(7), 12–18.

Kamil, M. L., Borman, G. D., Dole, J., Kral, C. C., Salinger, T., & Torgesen, J. (2008). *Improving adolescent literacy: Effective classroom and intervention practices: A practice guide* (NCEE 2008-4027). Washington, DC: National Center for Education Evaluation and Regional Assistance, Institute of Education Sciences, U.S. Department of Education.

Keene, E. O., & Zimmerman, S. (2007). *Mosaic of thought: The power of comprehension strategy instruction* (2nd ed.). Portsmouth, NH: Heinemann.

Lepper, M. R., Greene, D., & Nisbett, R. E. (1973). Undermining children's intrinsic interest with extrinsic reward: A test of the "overjustification" hypothesis. *Journal of Personality and Social Psychology, 28*(1), 129–137.

Lesaux, N. K., & Kieffer, M. J. (2010). Exploring sources of reading comprehension difficulties among language minority learners and their classmates in early adolescence. *American Educational Research Journal, 47*(3), 596–632.

Marzano, R. J., & Pickering, D. J. (2005). *Building academic vocabulary: Teacher's manual.* Alexandria, VA: Association for Supervision and Curriculum Development.

Marzano, R. J., & Pickering, D. (2010). *The highly engaged classroom.* Bloomington, IN: Marzano Research Laboratory.

Nagy, W. E., & Anderson, R. C. (1984). How many words are there in printed school English? *Reading Research Quarterly, 19*(3), 304–330.

Nagy, W. E., Anderson, R. C., & Herman, P. A. (1987). Learning word meanings from context during normal reading. *American Educational Research Journal, 24*(2), 237–270.

National Center for Education Statistics. (2010). *NAEP 2009 reading: A report card for the nation and the states.* Washington, DC: U.S. Department of Education.

National Governors Association Center for Best Practices, & Council of Chief State School Officers. (2010). *Common Core State Standards for English language arts & literacy in history/social studies, science, and technical subjects.* Washington, DC: Author. Accessed at www.corestandards.org /assets/CCSSI_ELA%20Standards.pdf on July 10, 2010.

National Reading Panel. (2000). *Teaching children to read: An evidence-based assessment of the scientific research literature on reading and its implications for reading instruction: Reports of the subgroups* (National Institutes of Health Pub. No. 00-4754). Washington, DC: National Institute of Child Health and Human Development.

No Child Left Behind Act of 2001, 20 U.S.C. § 6319 (2008).

Ouellette, G., & Sénéchal, M. (2008). Pathways to literacy: A study of invented spelling and its role in learning to read. *Child Development, 79*(4), 899–913.

Palmer, B. M., Codling, R. M., & Gambrell, L. B. (1994). In their own words: What elementary students have to say about motivation to read. *The Reading Teacher, 48*(2), 176–178.

Pearson, P. D., & Gallagher, M. C. (1983). The instruction of reading comprehension. *Contemporary Educational Psychology, 8*(3), 317–344.

Perie, M., Grigg, W. S., & Donahue, P. L. (2005). *The nation's report card: Reading 2005* (NCES 2006-451). Washington, DC: U.S. Government Printing Office.

Pressley, M., Allington, R. L., Wharton-McDonald, R., Block, C. C., & Morrow, L. (2001). *Learning to read: Lessons from exemplary first-grade classrooms.* New York: Guilford Press.

Pressley, M., & Wharton-McDonald, R. (1998). The development of literacy, part 4: The need for increased comprehension in upper-elementary grades. In M. Pressley (Ed.), *Reading instruction that works: The case for balanced teaching* (pp. 192–227). New York: Guilford Press.

Ramsay, C. M., & Sperling, R. A. (2010). Designating reader perspective to increase comprehension and interest. *Contemporary Educational Psychology, 35*(3), 215–227.

Rasinski, T. V., & Padak, N. D. (1998). How elementary students referred for compensatory reading instruction perform on school-based measures of word recognition, fluency and comprehension. *Reading Psychology, 19*(2), 185–216.

Rasinski, T. V., & Padak, N. D. (2001). *From phonics to fluency: Effective teaching of decoding and reading fluency in the elementary school* (1st ed.). New York: Longman.

Reardon, S. F. (2011). The widening academic achievement gap between the rich and the poor: New evidence and possible explanations. In R. J. Murnane & G. J. Duncan (Eds.), *Whither opportunity? Rising inequality, schools, and children's life chances.* New York: SAGE Foundation.

Rosenshine, B. (1983). Teaching functions in instructional programs. *Elementary School Journal, 83*(4), 335–351.

Samuels, S. J. (2007). The DIBELS tests: Is speed of barking at print what we really mean by reading fluency? *Reading Research Quarterly, 42*(4), 563–566.

Scammacca, N., Roberts, G., Vaughn, S., Edmonds, M., Wexler, J., Reutebuch, C. K., et al. (2007). *Intervention for adolescent struggling readers: A meta-analysis with implications for practice.* Portsmouth, NH: RMC Research Corporation, Center on Instruction.

Schunk, D. H., & Zimmerman, B. J. (1997). Developing self-efficacious readers and writers: The role of social and self-regulatory processes. In J. T. Guthrie & A. Wigfield (Eds.), *Reading engagement: Motivating readers through integrated instruction* (pp. 34–50). Newark, DE: International Reading Association.

Sénéchal, M., Ouellette, G., & Rodney, D. (2006). The misunderstood giant: On the predictive role of early vocabulary to future reading. In D. K. Dickinson & S. B. Neuman (Eds.), *Handbook of early literacy research* (Vol. II, pp. 173–182). New York: Guilford Press.

Shanahan, T., Callison, K., Carriere, C., Duke, N. K., Pearson, P. D., Schatschneider, C., et al. (2010). *Improving reading comprehension in kindergarten through 3rd grade* (NCEE 2010-4038). Washington, DC: National Center for Education Evaluation and Regional Assistance, Institute of Education Sciences, U.S. Department of Education.

Share, D. L. (2008). Orthographic learning, phonological recoding, and self-teaching. *Advances in Child Development and Behavior, 36,* 31–82.

Stahl, S. A., & Nagy, W. (2006). *Teaching word meanings.* Mahwah, NJ: Erlbaum.

Stahl, S. A., Heubach, K., & Cramond, B. (1997). *Fluency-oriented reading instruction.* Washington, DC: National Reading Research Center.

Stahl, S. A., & Heubach, K. M. (2005). Fluency-oriented reading instruction. *Journal of Literacy Research, 37*(1), 25–60.

Stanovich, K. E. (1986). Matthew effects in reading: Some consequences of individual differences in the acquisition of literacy. *Reading Research Quarterly, 21*(4), 360–401.

Strambler, M. J., & Weinstein, R. S. (2010). Psychological disengagement in elementary school among ethnic minority students. *Journal of Applied Developmental Psychology, 31*(2), 155–165.

Taylor, B. M., Pearson, P. D., Clark, K., & Walpole, S. (2000). Effective schools and accomplished teachers: Lessons about primary-grade reading instruction in low-income schools. *Elementary School Journal, 101*(2), 121–166.

Taylor, B. M., Pearson, P. D., Peterson, D. S., & Rodriguez, M. C. (2003). Reading growth in high-poverty classrooms: The influence of teacher practices that encourage cognitive engagement in literacy learning. *Elementary School Journal, 104*(1), 3–28.

Thiede, K. W., Wiley, J., & Griffin, T. D. (2011). Test expectancy affects metacomprehension accuracy. *British Journal of Educational Psychology, 81*(2), 264–273.

Topping, K., & Paul, T. (1999). Computer-assisted assessment of practice at reading: A large scale survey using Accelerated Reader data. *Reading and Writing Quarterly, 15*(3), 213–231.

Wanzek, J., Wexler, J., Vaughn, S., & Ciullo, S. (2010). Reading interventions for struggling readers in the upper elementary grades: A synthesis of 20 years of research. *Reading and Writing: An Interdisciplinary Journal, 23*(8), 889–912.

Weiser, B., & Mathes, P. (2011). Using encoding instruction to improve the reading and spelling performances of elementary students at risk for literacy difficulties: A best-evidence synthesis. *Review of Educational Research, 81*(2), 170–200.

Yopp, H. K., & Yopp, R. H. (2000). Supporting phonemic awareness development in the classroom. *The Reading Teacher, 54*(2), 130–143.

INDEX

40 Reading Intervention Strategies for K–6 Students
Elaine K. McEwan-Adkins
This well-rounded collection of reading intervention strategies, teacher-friendly lesson plans, and adaptable miniroutines will support and inform your RTI efforts. Many of the strategies motivate all students as well as scaffold struggling readers. Increase effectiveness by using the interventions across grade-level teams or schoolwide.
BKF270

Rebuilding the Foundation
Edited by Timothy V. Rasinski
Teaching reading is a complex task without a simple formula for developing quality instruction. Rather than build on or alter existing models, this book considers how educators and policymakers might think about rebuilding and reconceptualizing reading education, perhaps from the ground up.
BKF399

RTI & Differentiated Reading in the K–8 Classroom
William N. Bender and Laura Waller
Transition from traditional whole-group reading instruction to the 21st century classroom using three innovations that dramatically improve elementary reading instruction: RTI, differentiated instruction, and technology.
BKF363

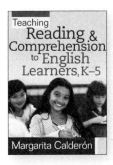

Teaching Reading & Comprehension to English Learners, K–5
Margarita Calderón
Raise achievement for English learners through new instructional strategies and assessment processes. This book addresses the language, literacy, and content instructional needs of ELs and frames quality instruction within effective schooling structures and the implementation of RTI.
BKF402

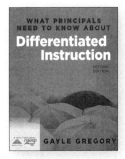

What Principals Need to Know About Differentiated Instruction, 2nd Edition
Gayle Gregory
This valuable resource gives administrators the knowledge and skills needed to enable teachers to implement and sustain differentiation. Learn information and strategies to jump-start, guide, and coach teachers as they respond to the needs of diverse students.
BKF536

Solution Tree | Press

a division of
Solution Tree

Visit solution-tree.com or call 800.733.6786 to order.

Solution Tree

Solution Tree's mission is to advance the work of our authors. By working with the best researchers and educators worldwide, we strive to be the premier provider of innovative publishing, in-demand events, and inspired professional development designed to transform education to ensure that all students learn.

The mission of the National Association of Elementary School Principals is to lead in the advocacy and support for elementary and middle level principals and other education leaders in their commitment for all children.